DOM MORAES (1938-2004), poet, novelist and columnist, is seen as a foundational figure in Indian English Literature. In 1958, at the age of twenty, he won the prestigious Hawthornden Prize for his first volume of verse, *A Beginning*, going on to publish more than thirty books of prose and poetry. He was awarded the Sahitya Akademi Award for English in 1994. He has won awards for journalism and poetry in England, America, and India. He also wrote a large number of film scripts for BBC and ITV covering various countries such as India, Israel, Cuba, and Africa.

Trained as an architect and city planner, **SARAYU SRIVATSA** was the editor of *Indian Architect and Builder Review*. Her book, *Where the Streets Lead* (1997), won the JIIA Award.

In 2002 she won the Picador-Outlook non-fiction writing award. Her first novel, *The Last Pretence*, was longlisted for the Man Asian Award in 2008. In 2016 her novel, *If You Look For Me, I Am Not Here*, was published in the UK, and was on the *Guardian* list for the Booker Prize.

ALSO BY DOM MORAES

Green is the Grass: Essays on Cricket (1951)

A Beginning: Poems (1957)

Poems (1960)

Gone Away: An Indian Journey – A Memoir (1960)

John Nobody: Poems (1965)

My Son's Father: An Autobiography (1968)

Mrs Gandhi: A Biography (1980)

Absences: Poems (1983)

Collected Poems: 1957–1987 (1987)

Serendip (1990)

Never at Home: A Memoir (1992)

Out of God's Oven: Travels in a Fractured Land, co-authored with Sarayu Srivatsa (2002)

The Long Strider: How Thomas Coryate Walked from England to India in the Year 1613, co-authored with Sarayu Srivatsa (2003)

A Variety of Absences: Collected Memoirs (2003)

Selected Poems, Ed. Ranjit Hoskote (2012)

Where Some Things Are Remembered

Profiles and Conversations

Dom Moraes

Edited by SARAYU SRIVATSA

SPEAKING
TIGER

SPEAKING TIGER PUBLISHING PVT. LTD
4381/4, Ansari Road, Daryaganj
New Delhi 110002

Copyright © Sarayu Ahuja, Executor of The Dom Moraes
Literary Estate, 2018.

First published in India by Speaking Tiger in hardback 2018

ISBN: 978-93-88326-70-4
eISBN: 978-93-88326-69-8

10 9 8 7 6 5 4 3 2 1

Typeset in Adobe Garamond by Jojy Philip, New Delhi
Printed at Sanat Printers, Kundli, Haryana

Contents

III
History and Happenstance

IV
Whose Eyes Witness

All history is a corridor of mirrors, in which adventitious images are recorded for posterity to accept or not to. All these images are to some extent distorted, not so much because of flaws in the mirrors as because of the enormous misconceptions that exist between person and person and between person and event. It is notably more difficult to write on somebody who is alive than on somebody who is dead. The dead are pinned down like butterflies under the lids of many cases, and in each case the specimen may be labelled and described. The researcher simply has to sift through the crumbled, lifeless squares of paper, select those which form some kind of pattern relevant to his own preconceptions, and there he is, his views in his head and the source material to support them at his elbow. When the people a writer is concerned with are alive, there is no question of neatly labelled, perpetually skewered specimens: groping through a giant haystack, he occasionally, and sometimes rather painfully, pricks his questioning finger on a needle. His hand may be septic in the end: but out of these myriad tiny pinpricks his book will be made.

DOM MORAES
1980

Introduction

We were at a restaurant with Dom's old friend, a Jesuit priest. He was attached to the St Xavier's College, and in his free time he was a sort of counsellor; he helped young people overcome their addiction to drugs and alcohol. He was rather surprised when he learnt that Dom hadn't had a drink in two years. He wished to talk to him about this. When he asked Dom how he had done it, Dom pointed to me and with a chuckle, he said, 'She controls me.' He had said this in jest but the priest took him seriously. When it was time for him to leave, the priest signalled me to walk to the door with him. Outside, in the street, he held my hand and said rather ominously, 'My dear, you must be careful. Dom is not an easy man; he can be very difficult and moody sometimes. And mind you, you must never forget that his mother went mad. It's genetic.' He placed his hand on my head as if to bless and walked away. Above the din of traffic I could hear the gulls cry over the sea.

'What was all that about?' Dom queried when I returned to him. He was rather intuitive and he could discern the disquiet on my face. I told him. His eyes fell to the nearly empty glass of lemonade. 'I could really use a drink now.' I reached out and touched his hand. He shook my hand away, irately, as if I was to blame. When he looked up at me his eyes were pained. 'I was always odd,' he said, 'and I never seemed to fit. People assumed there was something wrong with me. But when my mother was committed to a mental hospital people seemed to be certain of what was ailing me. Their unease turned to pity, and this was positively worse. I can't blame them though. I often worried if I would turn mad too. It was in my genes, after all. I did the next best thing: I got drunk. That was in my genes too. My father drank heavily.' I ordered us another round of lemonade.

It was only years after Dom died that I came across a brilliant book, *The Biology of Belief,* by Bruce Lipton, a renowned cell biologist. In this book he distinguishes between the world defined by Neo-Darwinism, which sees life as an unending battle of survival, and the New Biology, which is about a symbiotic journey. According to Lipton the cells in our body control their physiology and behaviour. A cell's life is monitored by its physical and energetic environment and not by its genes. Genes are simply molecular blueprints required to construct the cell. 'We are not victims of our genes,' Lipton asserts in his book. 'They don't define us; they remodel themselves in response to life experiences. The character of our life is based upon how we perceive it.'

There's a reason I mention this here; Lipton's discovery or analysis, as it may be, provided me with a blueprint to understand people, to empathize with them and the environment to which they belonged. Not that I succeeded at this. But this was something that Dom already knew and had honed. When he talked to people, or interviewed them, it was with a degree of humility, compassion and with utmost sincerity. Not because he knew anything about genes and cells but essentially because he could perceive and sense much beyond who these people were or what they said with the same temerity as he could sense who he was and was not. However, I must admit, he possessed deep prejudices about certain matters and particular kinds of people. These preconceptions were so entrenched that quite frequently he became rather irrational.

He was stubborn in a spoiled childlike way, and declined to be convinced or calmed.

The *Biology of Belief* is not a well-written book in a literary sense but the scientific facts are all there. The book may not have appealed to Dom but the discoveries within could have reassured him, dispelled his fears. The oddities in him, he could have assertively affirmed, were indeed a good thing. Dom often told me, what seemed to me then, odd and yet profound things connected to his own life, the lives of writers and poets, the choices they had, the decisions they made. Maybe they were wrong. Perhaps they were right. Either way, it hadn't mattered to them. This was important. It was the key: the oddness of it all.

★

In 1967, Arthur Koestler, a writer-philosopher, proposed the word *Holon* from the Greek word *Holos* (meaning whole) in his book, *Ghost in the Machine*. Koestler was a journalist who covered the Spanish Civil War and World War II from the perspective of ordinary people. After the war he turned to writing books in which he explored the inner worlds of experience and imagination.

According to Koestler, in a given natural and social hierarchy, Holon is a part and a whole at the same time—a part-whole. A Holon is a nodal point in a hierarchy. It is influenced by the character and environment of the larger whole it is a part of, and influences the smaller parts it contains. A word, idea, sound, an emotion are linguistic Holons—they are simultaneously part of something, at the same time have their own purpose and role; much like the nested Russian Matryoshka dolls contained within each other.

In Dom's own life, in the hierarchy of his relations over time: family, friends, lovers, writers, poets, within the smallest and yet deepest of connections, his mother is the Holon between

Dom and his writing. Each endured because of the other. The reason is ever obvious in that anyone who writes about Dom cannot but help write about his mother. As did Dom.

> *From a heavenly asylum, shrivelled Mummy,*
> *glare down like a gargoyle at your only son,*
> *who now has white hair and can hardly walk.*
> *I am he who was not I.*

In this collection of Dom's People, each person is a part and a whole, both special and strange, who were all swept up, one way or another, across order and chaos, in the social tumult of the country. As Marcel Proust's narrator says, in *Remembrance of Things Past*, the only true voyage of discovery is 'to possess other eyes, to behold the universe through the eyes of another, of a hundred others, to behold the hundred universes that each of them beholds.' The Nigerian writer Chimamanda Ngozi Adichie talked about the danger of a single story. It was about what happens if people and situations are reduced to a single narrative. Each individual life contains a heterogeneous compilation of stories. By reducing people to one, we take away their true and distinct identity. This book beholds innumerable universes through the eyes and words of many diverse persons, their varied stories, uncensored, and without judgement.

There was one aspect that was common in many of the people irrespective of their economic status, education and cultural backgrounds, which was immediately obvious to me, though not so much to Dom. It was the manner in which they related to me. We had interviewed people together and written about them separately in the sections of the book we co-authored, *Out of God's Oven*. Most of the interviewees assumed I was his assistant who took notes, and helped him in some small way or another. This was not entirely just because he was a famous writer and they were in awe of him, or that he was older and therefore wiser and more knowledgeable than me. It was more to do with gender. More than once the woman of the house asked me to help in the kitchen with the tea and leave the men alone to talk about serious matters. In one kitchen, funnily enough, I even submitted to frying samosas. In Lucknow, our journalist friend Nasser Abed said to me when he took us to meet a nawab, 'Sorry Sarayu, but I won't introduce you. If I do the nawab won't take the book Dom and you are writing seriously.'

Needless to say, I was peeved. When I complained to Dom, he said, 'I warned you didn't I?'

He was not wrong. I had published a travel book about twenty Indian cities but this was from an architect's point of view. I had suggested to Dom that we write a book together about India from different people's perspectives. He refused. 'I have never collaborated with anyone except with photographers,' he said. We observed things differently, I told him, as I was completely entrenched in all things Indian, and he was not; he was an outsider. Our perspectives would be different, which would be a good thing. After much persuasion he agreed but warned me that writing with him would have its drawbacks. I didn't believe him then. I did so later.

We were in Kolkata for the launch of *Out of God's Oven*. The newspapers sent their senior journalists to interview us. Many of them wanted to do an article about Dom, and the book. I was 'wallflowered'. Then one morning a young woman arrived from the *Telegraph*. She asked Dom why he had chosen to write with me. 'There are so many good writers, why her?' I beamed, looked eagerly at Dom. His reply was not what I expected. He told her he had chosen to write with me because I was a complete insider, that I reflected the culture and the deep past of India. He, a stranger to the country, was an outsider. We made a good team. I stood up. 'I love Kolkata sarees, I am going shopping,' I said and departed through the door.

When I returned with my purchases, thankfully the woman had left but Dom was miffed. 'You have to learn to behave,' he barked. 'You have to be professional and responsible. If you have written a book you darned well try and promote it.'

'Well, you could have told her I was a good writer. You have said so to me,' I snapped. At once Dom displayed his cheeky smile. 'I told her that because it would be good for the sales of the book. Did you get some good sarees?'

★

When he was not writing books or verse, Dom wrote columns for newspapers. He wrote profiles of people for a Sunday edition. They were about eminent people he had known or met, mostly poets, writers, and artists of the West. He didn't often write about musicians; he was tone deaf. He wrote of a time and place that many of his readers couldn't relate to; they read his columns anyway, as they loved the way he wrote them. The profiles and sketches included in this volume appeared in Dom's memoirs, other non-fiction books, anthologies and magazine and newspaper articles published over almost half a century—from the late 1950s to the early 2000s.

Dom would get flustered if he couldn't think of someone to write about, and his editor would suggest some important person in the city, even though utterly dull, or someone who was visiting it, or passing by.

One morning I found Dom sitting by the window. The obese goldfish in the fishtank on his windowsill made fishmouths at him. He had named the fish Gorky, the same name he gave the cancerous lump on his throat, both plump and growing. Strewn at his feet were pages for his Sunday columns for the month. A page, like a leaf blown, lay at the corner of the room. It was a sonnet of the last poem he had written—twelve sonnets that anagrammed his entire life. I stooped, picked it up, read the verse aloud:

Why does your bloated corpse cry out to me
that I took from the hospital three days dead?
I'd have come before, if the doctor had said.
I couldn't kiss you goodbye, you stank so much.
Or bear to touch you. Anyway, bye-bye, Mumsie.

Dom turned to me. 'I am awfully tired of writing these bloody columns. I don't know what to write or about whom.' He held his head in both his hands. He looked weary.

I suggested that he write about ordinary people; his readers would easily relate to them and their lives, and there were billions of them around. Like Mary, the widowed cook, who plied Dom with mutton 'chaaps', that he so disliked, and whose only son had squandered her savings in a ponzi scheme. 'Why do we have children?' she had asked. Or the fruit-seller who, wedging his foot between the door and the jamb, compelled Dom to buy an obese papaya each day. Dom preferred English fruits. The fruit-seller promised to get them each day. Or the night watchman who borrowed books from Dom to keep him awake through the night. Or the fishman who came to clean the fishtank, and swore to get a companion for Gorky. They all had an interesting past, I realised, when they started talking about it, and even more of a curious present. I was surprised when Dom readily agreed to write about them; his cancer was eating him.

Dom died in his sleep. The morning after Mary didn't come. It was her day off. The fruit-seller arrived ironically with apples. The fishman came rushing in with a goldfish, small and gaunt. 'I heard the sad news,' he said. 'I didn't give him his wish when he was alive, so I...' He didn't finish the sentence. He walked across the room to the windowsill and released the fish into the tank as though he was performing a funeral rite. The next day the night watchman came to return the books he had borrowed. I asked him if he would want a book written by Dom.

'Yes pliss, thank-u,' he said in English. His smile touched his eyes. 'Nice man sar was. Very nice.'

I gave him a copy of Dom's *My Son's Father*. 'You can read this for now. I will give you another when you finish this one.'

'I no read English,' he shook his head. 'The books sar be giving me just keep me company only.'

> *He laughs and after a short while I laugh with him.*
> *I realise, with a lump in my throat,*
> *that the comedy of our lives is not always divine.*

SARAYU SRIVATSA
Mumbai, November 2018

I

A Different People

Frank Moraes

Whenever I have visited London, after my father died, I have gone to look at the house where he last lived. This is a rather grand house in a Bayswater square. I look at the house for a while through the taxi window, before I ask the puzzled driver to go on. It is the only monument left to my father's loneliness.

The paper he had successfully edited for twenty years leased it for him when he announced to its astonished proprietor that he wanted, upon retirement, to go and live in London. He inhabited it with an American girlfriend, an Indian servant and four bossy little apsos bred by a Khamba warlord. But he lived in one room, alone. He seldom left it, even though the rest of the house was full of echoes of at least part of his past.

Objects that had associations for him reposed there: also thousands of books. Some dated back to his Oxford years. I had taken them from his shelves and read them when I was a child. Photographs filled every room except his: of him as a young war correspondent; of him laughing with Nehru, with various Indian and foreign prime ministers and presidents, and eminent friends. There were no photographs in any room, even in his own, of my mother or of me.

Last time I entered the house, nearly thirty years ago, I was passing through London on my way to New York, where I lived then. It was a fine autumn morning. The servant he had brought from Delhi, Saveri, opened the door. The apsos yipped shrilly in welcome; we had known each other since they were puppies. Saveri was a slight, dark young south Indian; he smiled at me with enviable teeth. 'Bada sahib is not okay today, sir,' he said. 'I take you upstairs.'

My father sat hunched at his desk. This stood by the window of his room, and overlooked the sunlit square. An untouched breakfast tray lay in front of him. Saveri had made his bed. In an adjacent shelf were stacks of Agatha Christie paperbacks and copies of all the books he and I had written. His face was unshaven and grey. He wore crumpled trousers and a cardigan. The apsos rioted round his slippered feet, ignored. He managed to smile. 'I didn't know you were coming.'

'Neither did I, till yesterday. I didn't have time to phone from Paris.'

'I have to write my column today,' he said with apparent irrelevance. 'The London office sends it home every Wednesday. I mean, to India. So it's lucky you came. I can't write because I have the shakes.' I had already noticed this, and also that he intended, or was required to write. My father always wrote in longhand, with a blue pencil, on sheets of rough paper, and his equipment lay on the desk in front of him, untouched like his breakfast. 'I've run out of liquor,' he said awkwardly. 'I don't like to ask Saveri. Can you get me some Teacher's?'

I did, from the off-licence round the corner. Ancient custom demanded that I poured his drink first, then mine. Then he put on his spectacles and started to write. The more he wrote and drank, the less his hand shook. Once he had finished and checked his piece, he sat back and sipped his whisky slowly. I hadn't seen him actually smile for years, but at least he didn't look unhappy. He looked tired, but pleased to be with me, and I like to remember him like that, for it was the last time we met before he died.

My father first came to England in 1927. He returned to Bombay ten years later. During this time he got a First in

History at Oxford and took silk at Lincoln's Inn. His father wanted him to be a lawyer. This was not only a safe but a very popular profession in British India. Gandhi, Nehru and Vallabhbhai Patel, the three great nationalist leaders, had all become lawyers in London and come back with novel Western ideas, such as democracy, human equality, and the concept of India as one country, which they felt should be freed from British rule.

My father admired these people, to the dismay and disapproval of his father, a civil engineer profitably employed by the British government. It was not the only occasion that the son defied the sire; one could say that he made a habit of it. Before he left for England, he became engaged to a girl who was at college with him, Beryl D'Monte. She was a Roman Catholic like him, but from a different community. My father's family came from the Portuguese colony of Goa. My mother's people came from around Bombay and were for some reason called East Indian. Both communities and both my grandfathers disapproved of intermarriage. But, after ten years during which they never met, my parents still wanted to marry, and in 1937, enraging both their families, they did.

But the worst hurt of all for my father's father was that his son refused to practise law. Instead, he became an assistant editor in the *Times of India*. A British company owned this elderly and powerful paper. My father and another young man from Oxford were the first Indians ever to be appointed to the editorial staff. But my grandfather considered journalists to be men without morals, the lowest of the low. Had he had a son who was a lawyer, he would have been proud. But to have a son who was a journalist shamed him. He imagined that it made others laugh at him or pity him. Where he got this idea from nobody knew; but he had it, very strongly. He took as many years to recover from it as he did to recover from my father's nationalistic views, or from his marriage.

From my father's personal point of view, his position as one of the first Indian editors in the *Times of India* had its invidious side. The English editors were provided with a luxurious room on the first floor where they lunched every day. They also had a lavatory to which each one had a key. The two Indians were at first not invited to lunch with the others, nor were they given keys to the lavatory. But some of the English editors were young men newly down from university, somewhat like those who had vowed at the Oxford Union, around that time, never to fight for King and Country. They told the management that the Indians should be given the same privileges of ingestion and excretion as the other editors, and if this were not immediately done, threatened to resign.

The management obeyed, and was also made to apologize to the two young Indians for the initial delay. My father never forgot this as long as he lived.

★

He was not a tall man, but in his youth, very handsome. His features were chiselled like those of a 1930s Hollywood hero; but he had intelligent eyes. My mother was little and pretty, with a clothes sense that was remarked on by her contemporaries. She was a pathologist, a consultant at a large hospital, and also attached to a laboratory. They looked good together and it would seem that they were much envied. She was garrulous and witty; he was much quieter, but had a dry sense of humour. By the time the war broke out they had collected a circle of brilliant friends, including Nehru. By that time, in 1938, I had been born.

We lived in a flat that faced a large park, the Oval. It was always full of people, for my parents liked to be visited. Some of them were English. Verrier Elwin, the anthropologist, came whenever he left the central Indian forests to collect funds for his work. He had very blue eyes and white hair; he chain-smoked cigars and drank formidable amounts of Scotch. Other guests usually included Congress workers or Communists. Some, hiding from the police, usually spent the night in my nursery. My parents never hid the fact that they were nationalists. It must have embarrassed my father's British employers.

In spite of this, when the Japanese attacked Burma in 1942, the paper made him the first Indian war correspondent, and sent him there. I don't remember much about his absence, save that my mother became unkempt and silent. She spent many hours listening to Negro spirituals on the gramophone, and crying. At this period Stilwell's army was in retreat from Burma and there was only irregular news of my father. He returned to Burma with Stilwell, and after that was sent to China. Altogether he was away for a very long time.

Towards the end of this time I had become adult enough to realize how miserable I was. I missed my father badly, and may have thought he would never return. But my mother caused most of my unhappiness. Huddled wordlessly in a corner, she seemed to emanate grief, like a vapour; and her terrible silences sometimes alternated with fits of astonishing violence when she broke dishes, attacked the servants, and screamed continuously in a voice I did not know. A friend had informed her that my father was having an affair in Burma.

When my father at last returned from the front, I was incredibly happy, but even that didn't last more than a day. All the complex combinations of silences and inexplicable violence that had built up in my mother over months ignited and exploded. Our flat was suddenly filled with agitated doctors and nurses, and weeping relatives. She was locked into her bedroom and I wasn't allowed to see her. Even my father could not tell me what the matter was, perhaps because he couldn't explain it to himself, perhaps because he couldn't accept it. But from overheard snatches of conversation between the servants, I gathered that my mother had gone mad. I knew what that meant, but at my age it was difficult to connect it with my once pretty mother, or with any other part of the life I had led.

★

In 1946, soon after my mother's first collapse into insanity, he was offered the editorship of the *Times of Ceylon*. We moved to Colombo and there my mother, who had made a temporary recovery, regressed a second time. She attacked me with a knife. After this my father took me with him to the office until he could find me a school. But my mother, estranged from him, and exceedingly unstable with me, yearned for India and her relatives. Her sister very reluctantly agreed to take her in. But the doctors didn't think it was safe for me to be with her, and so when my mother returned to India, she went alone.

Like any other child, I was naturally cruel and obsessed with my own needs. I felt intense relief at my mother's departure. I did well at my new school; my father spent all his spare time with me. He may have wanted to compensate for all the months he had been away. He gave me whatever I asked for, not only books, but a pair of cocker spaniels, budgerigars that bred happily in a cage the size of a cowshed, tanks full of tropical fish, and a pet turtle. But constantly, through letters and telephone calls, my mother's relatives asked my father to send me back to India. They said she needed me there for her mental stability.

My father replied that he was worried about my mental stability, if I went back now. I was tugged at from either side. I dreaded the idea of going back to India. I thought if I went back I would die. Lawyers were called in. At last my father succumbed to pressure and sent me back to Bombay, where I had to stay with my mother, in her sister's house. I felt like Lucifer, suddenly pitched from heaven into hell. For me this was hell, and I had to live in it. Day after day, I wrote to my father, begging him to come and save me. One day he resigned from the *Times of Ceylon*, and came back to India with my cocker spaniels.

He became the editor of his old paper, the *Times of India*. One of his first tasks was to have lunch with his new proprietor. The British company that had owned the paper for more than a century had sold it to an Indian textile magnate, Dalmia, who spoke no English. An interpreter was present when the new proprietor and his editor met. Dalmia was served his vegetarian repast on silver dishes. My father received his in earthenware utensils, later broken in the courtyard outside, in case they polluted Dalmia's caste. My father noticed this. He had never forgotten the young English editors who threatened to resign from the *Times of India* because he wasn't allowed to eat with them. The incident with Dalmia was another incident he never forgot. It was the first indication he had of what independent India might turn out to be like.

Dalmia, soon after he took over the *Times*, was imprisoned for tax evasion. His relatives, who wanted to please the government and constantly obstructed my father's editorial policies, inherited the paper. Given what he also had to face at home, I cannot imagine how he functioned in those years.

We had acquired a very large and beautiful flat by the sea. It overlooked green lawns where children played, and a swimming pool. My mother turned it into an arena for her demons. She prowled around in her nightdress all day. Her hair had turned white though she was not yet forty, and it stood up around her skull like a fright wig, never combed or brushed. The servants stayed as far away from her as they could. She became violent whenever she saw my father; so he left home very early and returned very late. She did not want me to see him at all. He and I could only meet for an hour or so every day, furtive as denied lovers, at restaurants or hotels, or even in his office.

I was by now going to school, which helped keep me out of her way. But I had now also started to feel an obscure but powerful need to write poetry. This required that I sat still with a pen and paper in one place, which had of necessity to be my room. I would lock the door and write, listening to my mother's slippers flap and slap outside as she went from end to end of the flat as though on a treadmill. My father's friends advised him to commit her to a mental home where she could be treated. He didn't want to, because he had loved her; and even had he wanted to, her relatives wouldn't have let him, because of the family name.

One morning my mother seemed to decide on a course of action. My father had left for the office. She locked the servants out of the flat, which also meant she had locked me in. As I watched, she began to fling the furniture out of the windows. She was tiny and frail, prematurely old, but she picked up heavy tables and sofas and tossed them around like matchboxes. I phoned my father's office. She paused in her activities, came up to me with a preoccupied look, and ripped the connection out of the wall. Then she went on with her work.

I locked myself in my room. I was still there when my father arrived with a squad of nurses and doctors. Next came the police, summoned by the neighbours. It was no longer possible to hide my mother's illness. It had become a public matter. She was declared insane and flown to the asylum in Bangalore.

That was the end of my childhood.

Basu Bhattacharya

Basu Bhattacharya was a filmmaker. As a young man, he had worked with the legendary Bimal Roy, whose daughter he had married and later divorced. He lived in Bandra, in a flat on the first floor of a small house dwarfed by the high-rises around it. It faced mangrove swamps, the viscous, polluted Arabian Sea and Joggers' Park, round which fat people walked daily, pumping their arms and panting. All newly rich, they wore Nike shoes. Their cars waited for them outside the park fences. The poor stared at their exertions through the fences, and failed to understand their motivation.

★

Every day, at dawn, a group called the Laughing Club assembled at Joggers' Park. Its members believed that laughter was good for them, even if it was forced. Basu*da* was consequently roused from his slumbers very early by the hyena-like cachinnations of about a dozen people under his bedroom window. They went on for at least an hour, so he had no hope of going back to sleep.

But his flat had a very large, oddly shaped terrace that overlooked the park. It was roofed against rain, and crowded with potted plants and antiques. When driven from his bed by the Laughing Club, he would establish himself there, bare-chested, in a lungi. He would chain-smoke, drink tea and eat bananas, meanwhile moodily plucking the grey hairs from his chest and staring out over the park towards the sea. He resembled a Roman senator on a bad day.

Sarayu and I used to walk in Joggers' Park, after the Laughing Club had finished. So we always glimpsed Basu*da*, sombre amidst his potted plants, and waved. At first he simply waved back. One day he beckoned us up to the terrace for a cup of tea, and this became a daily routine. He had had a full and eventful life, and liked to describe it, because as he grew older, he had become lonelier.

His Bengali ancestors had been not only wealthy landowners but priests. As a young man he had run away from home, and become a Communist. However, he was jealously watchful of whatever money he had inherited and made. He employed two manservants, and was as autocratic an employer as any of his ancestors. The servants performed all kinds of services beyond what they were paid for. They were expected to massage him for hours if he was tired, and he threatened to beat them if his orders were not followed properly.

But most of his flaws were inherited. He was naturally generous and kind. He suppressed these qualities in himself, because few people he knew in India shared them. He would not admit that he had faults, or equally, that India had any. As a young man he had lived for long periods in villages, some of them tribal. Yet he did not seem to think that the people in them suffered. Perhaps he felt it was their natural lot.

'India is the most beautiful country in the world,' he would proclaim. 'It has six seasons.' I could never work out what these seasons were, nor why Basu should consider it an advantage to have six of them. He also spoke often of the tolerance of Indians for other cultures. If the anti-Muslim riots of 1992 were mentioned he would reply, 'True Hindus would not harm Muslims.'

A Muslim family lived on the ground floor, under Basu*da*. A garden that showed evidence of much care flourished in front of their flat. When he sat outside with us, he was wont to throw his still burning cigarettes over the terrace wall, and they landed on the lawn or among the flower beds. He also spat, frequently and phlegmily, over the wall. When I remonstrated he said, 'Indians are tolerant. The man downstairs has only complained once, when my saliva fell by accident on his mother's head. He has seen my films and admires me.'

The Id festival took place, and the downstairs neighbours butchered a miserably wailing goat in their garage. Delicious smells of Muslim cooking rose to us as we sat on the terrace. Soon we saw a servant coming upstairs, carrying a covered silver tray. 'Ah,' said Basu. 'they are sending me a gift of mutton. In India your neighbours are always courteous and hospitable.' The tray was brought to him, and with a benevolent smile he lifted the cover. Underneath was a huge heap of mud-stained cigarette stubs. There was no message with them.

★

Baduda fell ill in the monsoon of 1997. First he became wan and withdrawn, then collapsed and went to hospital. The doctors found more ailments in him than I had imagined anybody's flesh could be heir to. When we last met he was lying in an antiseptic bed, needles like porcupine quills in his flesh. He tried to smile, but could not speak. A night or two later, he slipped into a coma, and died.

In the morning his corpse was brought home. Sarayu and I went to say goodbye. The garden outside was cluttered with mourners, for he had had many friends and admirers. A catering service busily dispensed tea in paper cups, and sticky sweetmeats. Innumerable pairs of shoes and sandals were strewed along the staircase up to the flat According to custom, they had been shed before their owners went indoors. A noise of Hindu chants and prayers came from upstairs.

There his closest relatives were seated on a capacious sofa. His son, who made films in Rome and had an Italian wife, had shaved his head as a sign of mourning. His daughter had come from Dubai. She and her younger sister, who had lived with Basu*da,* wore splendid silk sarees, but their eyes were red. Their mother, sourly divorced from Basu*da* for many years, sat with them as they received condolences. Smells of incense and flowers hung in the dank monsoon air.

Sarayu was welcomed into the room where Basu's body lay. The relatives at the door did not seem anxious to admit me. Then we bumped into Gulzar, the famous producer and songwriter. Thousands of Indians hum his songs every day; he could be called a folk poet. He is a Hindu but started life writing serious Urdu poetry and, like many others of his kind, adopted a Muslim nom de plume. 'I have been Basu*da*'s friend for twenty years,' he said. 'But they wouldn't admit me easily because I have a Muslim name. They won't admit you because you're not Hindu. All nonsense. Come with me.'

He led me to the door and, ignoring all protests, pushed me inside. Basu*da* lay on his bed, swathed in flowers. Only his Roman head was visible. His jaws were bound, and cotton wool sprouted from his ears and nostrils. Not knowing what else to do, I saluted the body and stumbled out once more.

Namdeo Dhasal

In the monsoon of 1997 a riot took place in Mumbai. It was in a remote suburb, Ghatkopar, in a Dalit settlement called Ramabai Colony, after Dr Ambedkar's widow. B.R. Ambedkar was the great leader the Dalits had needed through their 3,500 years of oppression. He has been dead for some decades, and the Dalits have more or less canonized him. His likeness stands in pink plaster at the entrance to the colony.

On a wet July night, unknown passers-by garlanded it with slippers. This deadly insult was discovered at dawn. The enraged Dalits spilled out onto the national highway nearby as though from a burst beehive, and started to pelt the passing cars with stones. A squad of armed riot police arrived. Two petrol tankers were parked off the road. For some unfathomable reason, the police officer thought the Dalits were trying to burn the tankers. He ordered his men to open fire.

Twelve Dalits, including two boys and a woman, were killed. By noon, every Dalit in Mumbai knew of this. Angry men with sackfuls of stone collected around the city. The police were out in full force. The offices closed early. When, towards evening, I needed cigarettes, all the shops were shut. In a commercial city, this was almost unheard of. The expected riots did not occur in Mumbai but in distant Ahmedabad. In Mumbai, isolated incidents of violence were reported. The atmosphere remained tense for several days.

At the end of this time I decided to visit the Ramabai colony. The leaders of the Republican Party of India (RPI), a conservative Dalit party, had been there. The residents of the colony, who felt let down by them, threw them out, but first beat them up. I badly needed someone with me who would be able to explain my presence in Marathi.

I phoned a friend, Rajendar Menen, a journalist who is also a student of Mumbai. He is a muscular, dark, handsome young man. He is also unusually resourceful and has many contacts. 'I know a restaurant owner in Ghatkopar,' he told me. 'I'll phone him.' Later he called back to announce success. 'He's shit scared of the Dalits, but he'll take us. I told him you wrote for the British papers, and you would write about him.'

Since I came to live in India I have shed many scruples. 'Fine,' I said. 'He speaks Marathi?' Rajen nodded. 'We'll start early tomorrow. It's quite a long drive.' He arrived on my doorstep at dawn; he had hired a car, and acquired a huge bunch of bananas ('In case Govind doesn't offer us lunch at his restaurant.'). Once we had left the city, we traversed faceless industrial suburbs, of which Ghatkopar was no more than a continuation. More trees grew here than closer to the city; once this had all been forest. Rajen told the driver to pull up in a puddled street, outside a gaudily painted cafe. The sign in front said 'Enchanting Restaurant'.

Under the sign, framed in a doorway hung with mauve-and-yellow strips of plastic, stood a man of about forty, in a blue raw silk kurta-pajama; though short he had contrived, like a pigeon, to puff himself up to look larger than he was. We clambered out of the car and shook hands with him.

His hand was wet and hairy. He said, 'I am Govind.' He indicated that we should enter. The interior was rectangular and contained three parallel lines of plastic tables and chairs, mostly occupied by diligent eaters. Waiters in off-white uniforms scuttered about as they came in. Govind indicated an empty table, barked orders, and disappeared into the rear of the restaurant. 'He won't come back till we've eaten,' Rajen said. 'It's his caste.' Steaming bowls and dishes appeared on the table. 'Better have lunch. It's Punjabi Chinese. Punjabi vegetarian Chinese. You may not like it, but eat it.'

I tried hard. 'I can see you don't like it,' Rajen said, not without slight malice. 'Elsewhere you might find Rajasthani Chinese, or Kerala Chinese.' He munched happily from a dripping spoon. 'As Nehru said, India is infinitely tolerant and absorbs all cultures.'

'Oh, be quiet, Rajen,' said I. 'What about the driver's lunch?'

'He's better off than we are. I left him the rest of the bananas.'

★

When we had finished, Govind came back, chewing heavily scented paan. He flumped down in a chair and asked me, 'In what British paper you will write my interview?' Rajen answered, 'In all papers, Govindbhai. Whatever he writes, all British papers print it.' Govind, deeply impressed, said, 'He must be well paid, isn't it?' Rajen smiled mysteriously.

'Sir, hear my views,' Govind said. 'Recently too much trouble has been made by these Dalits only. Now police are blamed for opening fire in Ramabai Colony. Why? Had they not, the Dalits would have set the oil tankers on fire and killed many poor people. I have said I will help you, but I also am nervous. Nobody can tell what such fellows will do. Not only they have no caste, they are without any kind of gentlemanly etiquette. They are very much lacking in good manners. They may abuse us and kick us.'

'Oh, I don't think so,' said I. 'We'll just try and be nice to them.'

Govind was piqued. 'Everyone makes excuses for these people,' he said, 'No good person can live properly because of them. See, sir, now they say they want to attend school and

college. Who has heard of such a thing before now? Low-caste
fellows who wish to be educated! And the Congress government
is conniving with them because it wants their votes only, isn't
it? So these Mandal reservations are made for them in schools
and colleges.'

The Mandal Commission, in the 1980s, had suggested that
a quota of places in educational institutions be reserved for
Dalits and tribals. Job opportunities were also provided by a
quota reserved for them in government offices. The government
of the time had turned the suggestions into law, in spite of
bitter protests from caste Hindus.

'They call them reforms,' Govind said bitterly. 'You don't
know what effect they had. In India you need a good degree
for a good job. Even when this Mandal business first came,
many children from caste families committed suicide. They got
eighty-ninety per cent in school finals, but the colleges would
not give them seats because they were too full of Dalits. Now
even, this happens. Our children are jumping from windows!
They are doing like monks in Vietnam, pouring kerosene on
self and burning!'

I flinched from the genuine grief and fury in his eyes.

'Now, less than before,' Govind said. 'Now there are options.
We can send our children to abroad, but that is very costly.
Why can they not find college places in their own country?
Why can they not be educated here?'

'Mightn't the Dalits and tribals have been saying that,
earlier?'

'Do they pay taxes, sir?' Govind demanded. 'Only *we*
pay taxes.'

★

We drove to the Ramabai colony. It seemed a sad, anonymous
little place to have caused so much uproar. As soon as the car
drew up outside, I realized that Rajen had made an unwise

choice of companion. For Govind changed indefinably, as though he had drawn on an invisible armour of caste. He stared with implacable disfavour at the dark, puny people who went in and out of the colony. He looked different from them, and was conscious of it. A gold watch glinted on his thick and hairy wrist. He was, in comparison with the Dalits, resplendently clad, and far better fed.

What I needed was to find a Dalit spokesman. But to achieve this, I had to depend on Govind, an interpreter who clearly did not want to interpret. A crowd had started to collect around our small group, and I did not think it looked friendly. Overhead the ragged rainclouds parted, and an incandescent sun pulsed slowly between them. It had become very hot, and I had developed a headache, which this absurd situation was not helping to cure. Then somebody took me by the arm and said in English, 'I am Vilas. May I assist you? Do you require something?'

He was a small, podgy man with a white moustache smeared over his upper lip. His khaki shirt and shorts gave him the look of a scoutmaster, and he appeared to have some authority in the colony. I said, 'I am a journalist. I wanted to ask about the incident here last week.'

'You mean the desecration of our leader's statue,' Vilas said, 'and the police firing?' He spoke English well, with familiarity. 'I think you don't speak Marathi?' He glanced at Govind. 'But *he* should speak his own language, isn't it?' He addressed the crowd briefly in Marathi. It dissolved. Vilas put a possessive hand on my shoulder and led me into the colony. Rajen and, far more slowly, Govind, followed us into one of the tenements.

We ended up seated on a rope cot in a small, well-scrubbed room with colourful calendars on the walls. Vilas sat opposite on the floor. Several people, including two women, occupied the surrounding area. 'First,' said Vilas, 'take some water. It is a hot day, is it not?' Steel tumblers of refrigerated water materialized. Rajen and I drank, but Govind wouldn't touch his tumbler.

Vilas observed this without remark. His eyes were very intelligent, and he took over the role of interpreter smoothly, and without resistance from the previous incumbent. Govind, finding himself surrounded by more people of low caste than he had possibly ever seen together before, had entered a catatonic stupor. More steel tumblers were fetched, containing tea. Biscuits and sticky cakes were handed round. But a glaze came over Govind's eyes, and he refused everything offered. He didn't utter a word, simply shook his head.

Meanwhile several people attempted to speak at the same time, recounting the events of July 10. They denied that anyone had tried to set fire to the oil tankers, 'though it was suggested by some boys,' or that the police had issued any warning before they started to shoot. 'They shot to kill,' Vilas said calmly. 'All those hit by bullets were hit in the body.' The others seemed angry, but also to expect and accept that there would be no redress: the incident would be forgotten by the outside world. 'No laws to protect us ever existed before,' said an elderly, shrivelled woman, 'and who will enforce them now? The caste people rule. They have always ruled.'

She had come to Mumbai forty years ago from a small town in Maharashtra. 'There when I was a girl, I did domestic work in the houses of caste people. The caste men wanted all the young Dalit girls to work in their houses. They said that if we touched them they would be defiled, but they all wanted us to touch them, and they wanted to touch us. Who was there to defend us?

'Our men could not protect us,' she said with sadness. 'There was nobody to complain to.' This, at least, she felt was no longer true. 'Now the caste people are afraid of our men. The government has made it possible for us to send our children to school, and then get work.' She meant through the

Mandal reforms that Govind had denounced. 'Mostly Dalit ladies are too much pleased with the reservation system,' Vilas said. 'We men are not so happy. It is too much a humiliation. We are looking even lower to the Hindus when we accept such things from the government.' Though he did not seem a fervent Buddhist, he denied that the Dalits were Hindus.

'It is a terrible religion,' he said, looking reflectively at Govind.

Clearly, more than anything else in the world, Govind wanted to leave; so clearly, that he had become an embarrassment to me. So I rose. The others followed me back to the car. Vilas handed me a scrap of paper. 'My telephone number,' he said. 'Perhaps we may talk some day. Are you knowing one poet, Ghodge? He was too good in Marathi, he wrote many songs for the Dalit people. But this police firing, it depressed him too much. He lived here in the colony. After the firing he hanged himself.

'We found his body only two–three days ago, by the smell, you know. We are sad that he has passed away, since he was one of us. Once another poet, Namdeo, Namdeo Dhasal, was with us, one of us, but now he is not there.' I questioned him. 'No, sir, he is not dead, except to us.'

★

'Where would I find Namdeo, do you know?' I asked Rajen.

Rajen said, 'From what I hear, he overdrinks and always needs money. He's now associated with the Shiv Sena. It suddenly wants Dalit votes. He won't be much use to them. Most Dalits feel he's betrayed them. I'll find him.'

★

It wasn't Rajen who found Namdeo, but Sarayu. The Marathi writer Shanta Gokhale, a friend of hers, arranged for us to meet him at Mantralaya, the Maharashtrian Parliament.

Namdeo, to my surprise, was an elected member of the Legislative Assembly. When we arrived at this large and unprepossessing edifice, a policeman said we couldn't come in without a pass. Whomever we had an appointment with should have provided one.

It was oppressively hot. Sarayu said irritably, 'See, it's already midday! I'll try and phone Namdeo. I've got his mobile phone number.' I found some incongruity in the idea of an oppressed and ill-treated Dalit poet who possessed a mobile phone. We went to the nearby Oberoi Hotel to call him.

'He says he can't understand what happened,' Sarayu reported, 'but he wants us to come back to Mantralaya and he says he'll wait at the entrance. We won't be able to miss him, he says, because he'll be sitting in his blue sports car.'

She did not miss my expression, and added cruelly, 'Your rebel poet seems to be a peculiar kind of Dalit. But he says he can understand some English, so now you had better speak to him.' A deep, gentle voice said 'Hullo.' I spoke loudly and enunciated my words clearly, like a British colonial official in conversation with an African chief. Would Namdeo please come to the Oberoi, at once? We could talk there. Namdeo, if this was he, replied, 'Very fine. Good evening.'

I wondered whether I had offended Namdeo. The four words he had actually uttered could be interpreted in different ways. But my delicate sensibilities misled me. Half an hour later, as I scouted the lobby, I saw a group of men waggling a placard with the name Tom Morris scrawled on it. I made a shrewd guess and approached them.

They were small, rather tense young men in well-pressed shirts and trousers. Gaudy ties were attached to their shirts, and mobile telephones to their belts. They had pale indoor skins and innocent little paunches and did not look like the other Dalits I had seen. This was prejudiced of me, perhaps. Why should all Dalits look deprived?

I introduced myself and they shook hands effusively. I inquired if they were Dalits. I regretted the question as soon as I asked it. Their faces froze, then slipped into expressions of absolute shock and horror. They were so deeply insulted that they didn't even bother to answer. Instead, they pointed to an older man who stood behind them.

He was short like them, but with dark, blunt features and a gritty stubble of grey beard. He wore a brown khadi kurta, loose white pajamas and leather sandals. He seemed different from his companions, even in the sense that they didn't look wholly out of place in the Oberoi lobby and he did.

'He is Namdeo,' they said. Then they closed round him protectively. In this new proximity, they and he seemed even more different from one another. I realized that they were his guards, rather than his companions. I suggested to Namdeo in English that he should come to the Lancers' Bar.

But Namdeo inquired, also in English, 'Where is Madam?' Madam, I said, awaited us in the bar. Namdeo shook his head, and gestured towards his clothes, presumably to show he wasn't dressed for the bar. He then said regretfully, 'Next day.'

One of the young men said, 'He will give you fixed appointment for tomorrow only. We will write down time and place.' Namdeo and some of the others then crowded round one end of the reception counter, first deep in discussion, then laboriously writing something down on a piece of paper. This took some minutes. Meanwhile one of them came up to me.

'Tom Morris,' he said reflectively. 'From what country you are?' I replied, 'I was born in India.' My slowness to comprehend him annoyed the young man. 'India, yes,' he said, 'but in India from which country?'

I said, 'Bombay. Or if you prefer, Mumbai.'

This information had a great and immediate effect. The young man gasped, 'Mumbai? You were born in Mumbai? But to what college you went here?' I said I hadn't been to college in Mumbai.

The young man said with pity, 'No, that I can see. In Mumbai the colleges are very good. But you are neither speaking Marathi nor Hindi and your English speech cannot be easily understood, as ours is. For this reason only I am asking from where you come.'

Namdeo and the others returned from their labours. I was given a slip of paper, on which an address in Mahalaxmi, and a telephone number were scrawled, together with the sentence, 'Appointment granted between 12 noon and 1 p.m.'

Next day we arrived punctually to keep it, at a tumbledown tenement in a slum lane. The front door was open. A young man who hadn't shaved appeared and said that Namdeo was at his home in distant Andheri. He wasn't expected here at all.

We retired defeated to a restaurant in Worli, not far off. Sarayu telephoned her friend Shanta Gokhale and told her what had happened. 'She says he's always been unreliable,' she reported to me. 'Now she says he's more so. He travels around with a group of Shiv Sena people, but the only person who has any control over him is his wife Mallika. Shanta's still friendly with her. She's going to phone Mallika up and ask her the best way to fix this appointment.'

Later she talked to Shanta once more. Namdeo's wife had said we should come next morning, preferably before ten. 'Because,' Shanta explained, 'he goes out at ten. After he has left home there's no way she can control him. She refuses to be responsible for what he does then.'

I had started to feel guilty. Vilas had implied that Namdeo had abandoned his people when they most needed him. Rajen had said bluntly that he had sold out to the Shiv Sena. Shanta had called Namdeo unreliable; his wife, in relation to how she handled him, had used the words 'control', and 'responsibility'; and Sarayu implied that his apparently chronic inability to keep appointments was only to be expected from a Dalit. My reaction was predictable. I began to feel like Namdeo's only protector in an insensitive world. I read a little of his poetry in Dilip Chitre's translation and some poems seemed to me remarkable. I now had a curious reason for our coming meeting. I wanted to apologize personally for everything that I had listened to about him. Of course, I also knew I wouldn't, in the end.

★

Lokhandwala is a residential colony in what were once the wetlands of Andheri. It has its clones in other parts of India, huge residential dormitories created from need, direct results of urban overpopulation. How Namdeo Dhasal, Dalit poet, had ever found his way into this labyrinth of new money, puzzled me as much as his mobile telephone, his yuppie escort and his blue sports car.

His flat was in a concrete anthill called 'Florida', aptly named perhaps: for most of the other tenants looked as though they had retired from active life many years earlier. Namdeo's landing held two flats. One had a firmly shut door. The other stood open, and we turned to it. Before we could ring, a dark, heavily built, stern-faced woman appeared, dressed in a blouse and a long skirt, presumably Mallika, Namdeo's wife.

I already knew that Mallika had a Muslim father and an upper-caste Hindu mother, and, which seemed highly likely, that she had endured various stresses in her marriage. She had written a widely read book about it entitled *Why I Destroyed My Life*. She pointed us to a sofa, then wordlessly swished through a curtain into the rear of the flat, and vanished.

The curtain was pleated down one side. It stirred in the monsoon breeze, revealing a narrow corridor, with a bedroom at the end. The bedroom contained laden bookshelves, though I could see no bed. One wall of the small front room in which we sat was covered with photographs of, perhaps, Namdeo's icons: Lenin; Ambedkar; the Maharashtrian reformer, Lokmanya Tilak. On another wall a framed certificate hung, written in Hindi: an award for poetry.

Otherwise the room accommodated two sofas and some chairs, a chintz-covered mattress on the floor, and a small desk in one corner. All it lacked was Namdeo himself. Mallika returned with a platter of biscuits and cups of very hot, very sweet tea. She still refrained from speech. I wondered if I should try and speak to her. For some reason I decided I had better not. Two men arrived, sat in the doorway, and following what seemed the household tradition, remained mute. I felt more than a slight despair.

But there was a scuffle of arrival outside. The two men who squatted on the landing didn't move. A third man, attached to a leash, and not Namdeo, was dragged through the door by a panting white Pomeranian. Mallika emerged from behind the curtain, and asked him a question. He shook his head.

Namdeo appeared behind him. He was dressed less confidently today, in a white shirt with a badly frayed collar and a checked lungi. Mallika snapped at him, obviously very annoyed. He made a small placatory movement with his hand, murmured. He was explaining his absence, saying that he had taken the dog for a walk.

★

Namdeo sat down on a very small chair beside the corner desk. The desk was also surprisingly small, and though not a large man, he bulked Gulliver-like amidst these Lilliputian items of furniture. His expression was also that of some contemporary Gulliver, trying to survive and feel secure in worlds not his. Possibly to encourage himself, he wore a smile so unreal that it embarrassed me.

He had spent his childhood in a small village near Pune, and attended primary school there, he told me. The Dalit children had had to sit and eat separately from the others. No Dalit was permitted to drink from the village well. When they bathed in the river, they had to be downstream from where the upper castes bathed. Namdeo had reacted against these customs. He started to write poetry early, he said, 'out of sheer humiliation.'

Namdeo said all this had happened towards the end of the 1950s, when Ambedkar's doctrines of equality had started to spread in rural Maharashtra. He had heard them discussed by his elders, and he had been a very responsive child. The Ambedkar movement had used the folk songs of the Dalits in their rallies. 'I started to write poetry,' Namdeo said, 'after I heard these ancient songs of my people.'

Namdeo's dark eyes flickered yellow. It occurred to me that he might understand more English than he admitted to. 'The community always had its folk theatre, its songs and its rituals,' he said. I often heard Marathi spoken in Mumbai, but it always sounded guttural, hawked up from the back of the throat, a language meant for vituperation. As Namdeo spoke it, Marathi had a flow and pulsation in it, almost like poetry.

He continued to explain Dalit culture. 'The Hindu caste system was first propagated about 5,000 years ago. Within the Hindu pantheon of divinities, untouchables always had their own deities, distinct from those worshipped by the upper castes. We had our own goddesses like Devamma, Mariaii and Yellamma, and our own gods. Some part of our prayers to them took the forms of devotional hymns, which is why there has always been a tradition of lyricism and song in the untouchable community.' I found it curious that he used the English word, *untouchable.*

Whatever the truth was about his desertion of his people, his mind seemed to dwell on them. 'If you look at Indian history,' he said, 'you find that when the Aryans came, a culture superior to theirs already existed. It had built great cities at Mohenjodaro and Harappa. The invaders attacked the people who had created this culture. They disappeared from history.' His thesis seemed to be that part of this pre-Aryan race fled into the forest and were now the tribal people. The rest, enslaved by the Aryans and put to labour so menial that the conquerors didn't want to do it, were now Dalits. No historical proof existed that this wasn't what had happened.

'Culture has to be diagnosed seriously,' he said. 'If we take an isolated part of it and develop it as a concept, we go astray.' His theory seemed to have evolved in precisely this fashion. But he was already in the midst of his next idea. 'When they talk of being a Hindu, it means nothing concrete. The Vedas, the holy books of the Hindus, were scattered, and only collected and presented in Hindu philosophy in the eighth century AD. Whatever ancient culture once existed was fragmented and made hybrid by the innumerable invasions of India.

'What now exists is a composite culture. The concept of simply 'being Hindu' does not exist. The Hindus are united only by hatred of another caste or religion. First they hated Dalits, now they hate Muslims. But they are the real outsiders in India.'

Namdeo was now showing interest in what he was saying, and he proceeded with it in the manner of some obsessive professor. 'When the Aryans came,' he said, 'they had chariots and horses. The non- Aryans had a superior culture, but they couldn't fight back. The Aryans were nomads who came from Persia, Afghanistan, Central Asia: they were outsiders. Those Hindus who take pride in them, those Hindus who assert that they are descendants of the Aryans, should be considered outsiders themselves.

'In this country there are 8,800 castes and 4,000 subcastes. Can you take this entire mass of people and call them all Hindus? And 22 per cent of them are Dalits, who themselves have their divisions. I am of the Mahar caste.' The traditional work of Mahars has had to do with dead meat and leather, with flaying, skinning and cutting up often nearly putrescent animal carcasses. The bulk of the converts to Buddhism were Mahars.

'Now,' said Namdeo, 'the right-wing Hindus are trying to band all these disparate elements together and say they are Hindu. It is a myth. They are trying to build Hinduism up into an aggressive force. India has accepted many conquerors who had superior weapons, and Hinduism became passive as part of a composite culture. Within that culture it had to accept its boundaries. Now that Hinduism is trying to redefine its boundaries, it will lose its way. The outcome of all this will be civil war.'

★

Meanwhile the two men sitting on either side of the front door, still open, followed the example of the Pomeranian, now recumbent at Namdeo's bare feet. They went to sleep. A young man, possibly Namdeo's son, came through the curtain and sat on the mattress by the wall, where he remained, not saying a word. An old woman slipped unobtrusively in, and sat at the other end of the mattress, also wordless. After a while, she rose and slipped out. A younger woman appeared at the front door, and stared silently and fixedly at Namdeo for some time, before she left. She was followed by another young woman, who wore lipstick and carried a handbag, insignia of modernity that she asserted by speaking to Namdeo. He replied without looking at her.

She also left. None of these people was introduced, nor did any of them seem to expect it. This wasn't typical of the Indian middle class with whom Namdeo now lived. But the open front door was not uncommon in Mumbai tenements, or in villages. It indicated commonalty. When the doors of the outside world were closed to the Dalits, they left theirs open, allowing free passage to one another.

'For many centuries Hindu society shut out the Dalits,' Namdeo said. 'They were not allowed responsibility, education or liberty. They were hated by the upper castes. It was not only the social system that propagated this, but religion. This was propagated by the Aryan caste system, even in the Upanishads. The lower castes were supposed to do filthy work and be denied education. This came from the Hindu concept of karmic cycles. You pay in this life for sins in a past life. Centuries passed before Hindu reformers looked at the sacred texts and said they had been misinterpreted. Then reforms were proposed and sometimes they were undertaken.'

Namdeo paused and lit a small beedi. His was more impressive in appearance than the normal variety; it was the kind made for export. 'Today,' he said, 'some Dalits are educated. Mostly they are aware of their rights. Ambedkar brought this awareness about, and now the Dalits are fighting for their rights. Today one could say that untouchability in its old form doesn't exist, at least in its physical aspects. But there are other harmful prejudices built into the Hindu mind.'

The Namdeo I had been told of had spent most of his youth in brothels and bars. But this squat dark man, quietly caught up in what he was saying, seemed learned, almost academic. 'The Dalits were forced into certain areas of work by the caste system and developed certain specialized skills. In a modern context these skills have been made redundant. Once the leather worker made waterbags for use in the fields. The Kirloskar sprinklers have now replaced these. That's only one instance.'

He continued, 'The government has introduced reservations, quota systems, for Dalits. That's a step forward. But it's not properly enforced. There are four grades of government employees; the lowest is the fourth. You will find a minute proportion of Dalits in the first three grades, but the fourth is full of them. That is the grade that does menial work. In schools and colleges, the upper castes have infiltrated the places meant for Dalits. The implementation of the reservation system is faulty.

'You have asked me what the word "Dalit" means. You know in Marathi there is the Sanskritized language and the language of the common people. This is a Sanskritized word that has become part of common speech, part of the language of the proletariat. It is parallel to the word "untouchable", but more forceful. It means "the oppressed". It means the oppressed of all castes and classes, even upper-caste people.' He paused and passed his hand tiredly over his face, a frequent gesture. Then he muttered an apology.

He crushed his beedi out in a small copper ashtray. The presence of ashtrays in the house seemed to indicate Mallika's hand. Namdeo as a young man had lived a rough life in Mumbai; he had not been brought up to such niceties. I trusted that the cheroot had soothed his nerves, and asked a question that might annoy him. 'I went to the Ramabai colony. The people there were mostly Mahars like you.' I hesitated. 'Unlike you, they are neoBuddhists.' Namdeo nodded dourly. 'They felt you betrayed them, forfeited their trust, when you went over to the Shiv Sena. Why should they feel this?'

Namdeo said that the Ambedkar movement in the 1950s had left the younger Dalits restless, wanting change. In 1960, Mumbai, previously an independent city-state, was made the capital of Maharashtra. At this time unemployment was chronic in the state. Outsiders monopolized the worlds of blue and white collars.

At that time, when he had helped found the Dalit Black Panthers, Bal Thackeray founded the Shiv Sena. 'The Republican Party of India, the RPI,' Namdeo said, 'was also a product of the second half of the 1960s, the first half of the '70s. It claimed to represent all the Dalits, but it was not representative. Meanwhile, the Dalit Black Panthers split up. I joined the RPI. It split up also. But the Shiv Sena became steadily more popular, it appealed to the Maharashtrian middle class. It was a product of the industrial revolution in India. It helped the sons of the soil.'

The Shiv Sena offered young Maharashtrians an outlet for their curbed violence, and turned them loose on the South Indian community in Mumbai, saying that they had exploited the city to make money. The Shiv Sainiks attacked the South Indian colonies in Matunga and other suburbs, looted shops, and killed a few people. After this, Bal Thackeray, the cartoonist who led them, decided on another policy: that of Hindutva, the union of the country by Hinduism. Now, three decades after his men first attacked South Indians, he incited them to attack those whose faces did not fit: Muslims and Dalits.

'Now the Black Panthers and the RPI have restarted,' Namdeo said. 'There is no question of an alliance between Dalits and Muslims. Both are oppressed minorities, but that is the only common point. Muslims are fundamentalists, and they also practise a caste system. Look at the Shias and Sunnis. Those who fight communalism are often communal themselves. We can only come together if they reform. We cannot unite with the RPI. It now only represents those who have become Buddhists.

'I want all the Dalits to be united. The Dalit Black Panthers were dissolved in December 1995, but now we're active once more and represent all classes. But the question that troubled me is 'What do you do when you have united the untouchables? Revolt against the upper caste?' We should establish a relationship with them instead.

'This is our manifesto. You can't break the caste system by fighting one caste. The BJP and the Shiv Sena consider us a powerful force in Maharashtra today. Our party represents the entire lower class. Ambedkar never differentiated between castes. He didn't hate Brahmins, only the way Brahminism was practised. He was very contemporary in his vision.'

He lit another beedi. He held it between forefinger and thumb, and cupped the lighted end in his palm, as peasants did in villages and on railway platforms, to shield the ember from the wind. 'But when we say what he said, we are attacked. No really strong individual Dalit party yet exists, because of these differences. I have said that one must first offer the untouchables a programme that will unite them, then integrate them with the upper castes so that we can fight economic and social problems together. We have to form a Dalit party where all communities are represented, even the upper-caste victims of oppression. Even if we ally with the Shiv Sena, our identity will not be weakened. They already have untouchables with them. In reality, all Dalits except the Buddhists of the RPI are with the Shiv Sena.'

At about this point, his face, until then impassive behind its beard, started to show expression. He gestured plaintively with his hands, as he had done much earlier when trying to pacify Mallika. His sentences came more quickly than before. 'I have not become a supporter of the BJP,' he said. 'I write for the Shiv Sena paper, *Samna,* but I attack caste conflicts. I am trying to bring about a reform within the Shiv Sena. Ours is a temporary alliance.' For my benefit he repeated the words 'temporary alliance', in English. He nodded vigorously as he said them, and smiled.

Before we left, I asked Namdeo whether he had written any new poetry. He had recently published a collection of it, he replied, and brought out two well-produced books in Marathi. One contained his poems, the other his essays from *Samna.* Not very much of his poetry had been turned into English, he said. But the poems were available, 'only in America' he added mysteriously, 'in French, Russian and German.'

In the end, what was truth? Pilate would never have found the answer in India. Here events took on diffused shapes that overlapped and faded into each other. Sometimes the truth could be glimpsed briefly, from the corner of an eye, like a rat that streaks across the floor and disappears. It was glimpsed, it has gone; nobody can tell you where it may now hide. The truth about Namdeo was like this.

Sunil Gangopadhyaya

In Kolkata, looking for a writer called Sunil Gangopadhyaya, I got lost in a maze of long tree-spiked avenues. They were lined with blocks of flats; this was a residential area for the upper middle class, who seemed not to believe in street names. By now the morning mist had lifted, and left an innocent village smell of wood smoke behind. I suggested in English to the driver, who spoke some, that he should ask for directions. The driver didn't want to. He felt the people here were too rich and proud to answer a poor man like him. 'Sir,' he said, 'please to ask them yourself.'

He pulled up beside an elderly man in a crisply pressed khadi tunic and dhoti. This representative of the bhadralok had a shopping bag in one hand; the other clutched a dripping packet wrapped in newspaper. Carrots lifted tufted heads from the bag; a not unpleasant smell of fresh fish and newsprint rose from the packet.

He stopped and stooped to the car window. I asked for directions. 'Addresses are of no use in Kolkata,' he replied in a Cambridge accent. 'But who is the person you want?' I told him. 'Ah, of course,' he said, and instructed the driver in what sounded like upper-class Bengali. I thanked him and said, 'We're lucky to meet you. I had no idea you knew him.'

'Why do you think I know him?' inquired the old gentleman. 'I am only a small person. I have never met him.

But every citizen should know where our famous writers live. Sadly, few are left since my friend Buddhadeva Bose passed on.' He inclined a courteous head and walked away.

I was still stunned when I met Sunil Gangopadhyaya. He gave an impression of bulk, with a heavy, tranquil, Buddha-like face. When he was told about the encounter, a mysterious smile came to it and he said, 'Once it wasn't rare to find such people in Kolkata. Now it has become rare. It's a great pity.'

His novels were widely read, though he was mainly a poet. He also worked on a newspaper. His flat indicated that he had, in terms of income, become part of the middle class, though he would perhaps prefer it otherwise. He is a Marxist, but not unreasonably so. The room where we sat contained books; a painting or two; the appurtenances of a Kolkata intellectual's life. He seemed comfortable in this life; perhaps a little taxed by its demands. He tried to explain his city.

'I remember the 1946 riots here. I was twelve then. Where we lived, in north Kolkata, there were riots in great magnitude. We watched Muslims killed on the streets. Nobody picked up the bodies and a terrible stench came from them. Then, after five or six days, rigor mortis set in and the corpses actually sat up. I saw them sitting up in rows, a horrible spectacle from our window.'

He talked slowly, in a meditative manner, unlike the ferocity and violence of his fiction and poetry in translation. 'At this time Mahatma Gandhi came to Kolkata to plead for peace. He had been to East Bengal, but could achieve nothing there; he was booed. He was stationed in a house near Beliaghat, a Muslim area. We Hindu school kids went to him and he insisted that we shared some water with the Muslim boys. We did and we were elated to have done it.

'When Independence came the older people were enthusiastic, but we were leftists in my family. We thought it was not really Independence and shouted slogans. "*Yeh azaadi jhooti hai:* this freedom is false." We expected all the war profiteers would be hanged from the lamp posts. But nothing happened. For my family, Partition was more important than Independence. Like many other families here, our old home was in the east and we lost all our land. Others were cheering. In my house, though we were leftists, we were crying.'

The weeping went on for years, Gangopadhyaya said. 'Until 1950 there were riots on both sides on the new border. These were retaliations, and many more were killed. And what sort of a border was this? Mr Charlton was sent from London to decide where it should be. He came here for fourteen days with his knife. He cut and said, "This piece goes to India." He cut once more and said, "This piece will be Pakistan's." The man had never seen these places, never known what kind of people lived there.

'As for the Congress leaders, Gandhi was right when he said they should have dissolved the party once Independence was certain. See how easily they accepted it all, Charlton's butchery, everything. They were not the kind of people who could run a country. Essentially they were agitators who were equipped to oppose authority, rather than hold it. Their folly caused great tragedies in Punjab and Bengal. Nehru was an idealist with the wrong ideas.

'He thought people had no religious bias. He was wrong. The division of Hindus and Muslims existed long before 1947. In Bengal, I know that the Hindus hated the Muslims. I saw the contempt with which my grandfather treated wealthy, educated Muslims. He made them sit outside his house; he wouldn't even give them water. There have been no major communal riots here for some years now. But there are few Hindu–Muslim marriages. How Nehru decided Hindus and Muslims could be friends remains a mystery.'

'But the BJP hasn't had much success in Bengal,' I said.

'Not yet. But the young people want a change. Some may

be inclined to the Left because of tradition, but they have no objections to the caste system and no interest in the class struggle. They're more materialistic than ever before. We have missed out badly on education. From the outset there was no effort to provide it. In other fields there is some slight improvement. For example, we are proud to be almost self-sufficient when it comes to food production.'

He paused for effect and continued, 'We ignore the fact that only 50 per cent of the population has the buying power to feed itself adequately. Many people still starve, and we cannot help them.' His lips twitched; he was laughing. 'Some people have expressed surprise that there has never been a large-scale peasant revolt in India. This is because of the Hindu religion. The godmen say you cannot escape your fate. If you were born poor, God meant you to starve all your life. If I were in power I would ban all religious activity.' He concluded with a sour expression, 'But hypocrisy is the Indian hobby, common to everyone.'

'Corruption is an offshoot of hypocrisy, the habit of lying to oneself. If bribery is banned, the machinery will cease to operate. If you don't keep up the corruption level, no task will ever be done. It's part of the tradition. As for revolutions, they need a leader. In this huge mass of people, where is there such a person? The situation is wrong. A revolution may create its own leaders, but it is also obliged to feed its own children. In addition, we don't seem to know what India is. There are movements in some states towards a separate identity. I really don't know.' He had a quality of reticence that was not Bengali. 'I don't want India to break up,' he said. 'But look at the flaws in the national character. We have an endless capacity for hero worship, but we also pull down our heroes. That is another aspect of our hypocrisy.'

He saw me off, smiling. 'I couldn't help you much,' he said. 'I think as you ask questions about India, you will find many other people like me, who will point out what is wrong. That is, of course, glaringly clear. But I don't think anybody will be able to point out a way to make it right. If he could, he would be a leader, and India's tragedy is that it has none.'

Mahashweta Devi

One afternoon I went to see the woman writer Mahashweta Devi. She is a reclusive figure, seldom seen by the media, but her novels and short stories have won immense respect. A taxi took me to a house in a tree-lined backstreet. A placard on the gate said 'Boarding House'. Beyond this was a ramshackle tenement, surrounded by flowering trees.

A precipitous spiral staircase in iron, painted red, climbed one side of the tenement. I eyed it with apprehension. I have suffered from acute vertigo since childhood. I decided to take this hazard at high speed, flung myself up the stairs, and burst dishevelled and panting into the room above. An elderly lady in a saree stared at me in shock. I identified myself. 'Yes,' she said, after a shaken pause, 'I was expecting you. I am Mahashweta.'

She had the manner of a friendly headmistress. Her room was small, and also friendly. It contained a desk occupied by papers and an ancient typewriter, two chairs and a cot where an orange tabby cat slept. 'She allows me to live here,' Mahashweta said. She sat at her desk. The tabby and I shared the cot. I had a strong sense of female dominance.

She had a quiet, sane voice. It retained the same even tone, whatever she was saying. 'When Independence came,' Mahashweta Devi said, 'we had to start from scratch. This was surely known to our leaders. What the people needed most then were land reforms. These were later done in the Communist states, West Bengal and Kerala, but not properly. The central government never even tried. In 1947, Nehru should have seen that there weren't enough roads, drinking water, healthcare, or schools. Nothing was done for those not already privileged. It has always been so.

'Fifty years later we're at a point of no return. Today India has an extension of a medieval value system where the lower castes, the tribals and women count as less than human. The privileged and powerful are the same as before, under different names. They're called industrialists now, not princes.' She had recovered from the shock of my precipitous arrival, and even become talkative.

'I live mostly in a district in north Bengal called Purulia. It has no roads, no drinking water, no land for the poor, and a large number of what the British called "criminal tribes". They are still treated as pariahs. They have taken my life. For twenty-five years they have been my life, and I am seventy-two. I work only on their behalf. I have written books and won awards because the class I come from is privileged. The people I work for never received privileges.'

The tabby cat beside me was a female version of Garfield. It showed the pink inside of its mouth in a yawn. It then stretched voluptuously and licked its chops. Its owner fixed it with a stern stare. I wondered who fed it when Mahashweta Devi was away, though it seemed well equipped to look after itself. So, indeed, did Mahashweta Devi.

'My grandson is educated and knows little,' she remarked. 'My son is the same. It happens; it's only natural. I know how villagers and the other underprivileged people live. Few others from the privileged classes can say that.

'I recently had to translate a book by Mahatma Gandhi. He was concerned about the Dalits, but the word "tribal" does not occur in this book. Gujarat, where he was born, is full of tribals. But it seems he did not notice them. He had strange ideas; he did not even know how poor people eat. The tribals will eat whatever is there. But Gandhi recommended that they should live on fruits, nuts and milk. He didn't know how much such a diet would cost.'

Mahashweta Devi has had to count her pennies in past years. Her husband was one of the founders of an important leftist movement of the 1940s, IPTA, the Indian People's Theatre Association, which took plays to the villages. 'I married at twenty. In my father's house I had no hardship, but after my marriage, I came to know what poverty, hunger and struggle were. That was my choice. I have always acted in an independent way. I think perhaps I am very stubborn.'

She wasn't very anxious to talk about her life. 'My main work is in Purulia with the tribals. All I want for each family is two meals per day, a hut to live in, an electric supply, some education. It's not much, but they haven't got even that. Do you know about the tribal development funds sent to each state? All I know about it is that it does not come to the tribals.' She spoke unexcitedly, aware that anger wasn't useful, it wasn't enough.

'I will try and go on fighting for them until I die, but it has become difficult for me to do all that I used to do. Once I covered the whole Palamau district in Bihar on foot. It is the most wretched place in India. There I saw the bonded labour system in operation. You could call it slavery. Then I went to Delhi, I fought for the Palamau people, and I wrote articles in a number of papers. Now we have some organizations for human rights there. Recently I read an article on activist writers. It contained some paragraphs about me. How much they surprise me now, all the things I have done.'

She sat quietly at her desk, the late afternoon sunlight luminous on her spectacles. 'The tribals are not as simple as people think. They know the ways of this country. If a local politician comes to Purulia and says he will build a road or a bridge, do you know what these illiterate people say? They say, "Elections must be near."'

Ramnath Goenka

In 1970, I became the editor of the *Asia Magazine* which enabled me to travel all over Asia. Thereafter, I was commissioned to write a book about Indira Gandhi on which I spent two years. In 1980, I found myself in London having lunch with my agent, Peter Grose. 'You have been away for too long,' he said. 'All your contacts here are gone.' He advised me to return to India. It sounded like a prison sentence.

I returned to Mumbai. I felt a version of the *Asia Magazine* could be started from Mumbai, it could go into the Asian papers. Regarding the financing for such a magazine, it seemed to me that a prospective proprietor would be tempted by the thought of earning badly needed foreign exchange.

After a good deal of looking around, I was approached by Ramnath Goenka, who owned and ran the *Indian Express,* my father's old paper. Goenka was now seventy-eight, an ancient maverick, and an avowed foe of Mrs Gandhi. His newspapers had attacked her fiercely during her period out of power. Now that she was back, he needed to be in her good graces. He had heard that I had written a book about her, with her collaboration, and possibly thought that he could come back to being one of her chosen, through me. He didn't know then that Mrs Gandhi and I had ceased to be friends since the book. When, slightly late, Goenka discovered this, he was horrified. But he felt he might still get some mileage out of me. He said that my magazine idea was excellent, and that he had colour printing machinery. He omitted to tell me that it didn't work. But he did tell me that it might take a while to get the magazine organized. He wanted me on his staff, he said, immediately. He offered me what for India was a stupendous salary, with various perks, and the editorship of the Sunday paper.

My cousin, Darryl D'Monte, was then the Bombay editor of the daily paper, and it was through him that I first met Goenka. Actually, I had met him before, in London. He had looked then, exactly as he looked now—squat, bald and powerful, with a small grey moustache that looked like a blister on his upper lip. He dressed, then as now, in a white kurta and dhoti, like most Marwaris, a class noted as industrialists and moneylenders. In London, Goenka had said that he wanted to improve the standard of English in the *Indian Express,* since, apart from my father, nobody wrote it well. So he wanted to employ several young British reporters as senior editors. I asked if my father knew about this. Goenka said he did. I gave a lunch party to which a number of candidates had come, as well as James Cameron, the Canadian filmmaker whose net worth ran into millions. James watched as Goenka talked to the young men, promising them much in the way of salary, accommodation and perks. When lunch was over, all of them, about half a dozen, had been recruited. 'But,' Goenka said to me later, 'that old man who was there,' he meant James, 'I want to hire him. I will pay him three times what I am paying these boys.' James laughed softly when he heard this, and advised me to phone my father to tell him what was happening. 'I wouldn't take that ruffian Goenka's word about anything,' he said. 'If he says he's told Frank, I'd bet anything he hasn't. All Frank's staff will resign when they hear about this.' Goenka, of course, hadn't told my father, who was furious. Only one of the young men selected ever reached India; he returned miserable, but toughened.

I remembered all this two decades later, when Goenka spoke to me in Bombay. But I accepted his proposal, and next day became the editor of his Sunday paper.

The *Indian Express* was published from about a dozen centres. Goenka himself divided his time between Madras, where he had a house, Delhi, and Bombay, where he lived in a penthouse above the office. He used to ask me to lunch in the penthouse, where the food was vegetarian. The first time I went to this place, he eyed me pensively for a while, then suddenly roared, 'Sack Monto!' I looked at him uncomprehendingly, for I didn't know what he meant. 'I am telling you,' he shouted, 'sack Monto!' He thumped his fist on his knee.

'Why should I sack him?' I asked. 'Anyway, who is he?'

'It is enough that I want you to sack him,' Goenka said. 'And what do you mean, who is he? He is Monto, I am telling you! Monto! Your own cousin, and you don't know him?' He meant Darryl D'Monte, whom I promptly told about this new development. I also pointed out to Goenka that I had no authority to sack Darryl, and wouldn't. For days after this he pointed out to me that I should not allow family considerations to come between me and my duty, which was to sack my cousin. 'You think you are being a gentleman,' he would thunder. 'Gentlemen never become rich. I have only seen one bigger bloody fool than your father, and that is you.' I found this amusing, but he meant it.

He made other peculiar demands. He once invited my wife Leela and me to dinner with him. The only other guests were the chief minister of Maharashtra, A.R. Antulay, and his wife. Antulay was a Muslim—a short, affable man, and a fervent supporter of the Congress party and Mrs Gandhi. He had so far, in his short tenure as chief minister, made an excellent impression on most people. He had set up a number of trusts which were intended to alleviate the condition of the poor in Bombay. In addition to this, he had begun to issue cement, of which there was a shortage, to industrialists willing to put up factories which would provide employment to unskilled labourers.

I did not know it at the time, but Goenka needed cement for his Delhi office, to which he was adding a new wing. He decided Antulay would provide it. Maharashtra was then producing surplus cement. He encouraged me to befriend Antulay. As a matter of fact, I needed no encouragement. I liked the chief minister. When Goenka advised me to 'write nicely about this fellow', I was prepared to do so. Eventually Goenka asked me if we could help Antulay in any way. Antulay said that he would like to meet some industrialists. I invited J.R.D. Tata and several other industrialists to a party in an expensive hotel. They were anxious to meet the new chief minister. Shortly after this, Goenka asked for a huge amount of cement, and Antulay turned him down, as he pointed out, it was illegal. Goenka called me to the penthouse flat. 'Attack Antulay,' he said. 'Finish the bloody Mussalman'. I refused. 'I'll pay for the researchers,' he said. 'With money, you can always dig up something.' When I still refused, he said, 'Your father was the biggest bloody fool I have seen. When I made such requests to him he also refused to obey. But he made the *Indian Express* a big paper. I needed him, so I didn't sack him.' A grey mildew of stubble smeared over his upper lip. Spittle dripped from his lower lip. He was shaking with fury, and looked simultaneously disgusting and comic. 'You are an even bigger bloody fool than your father. I don't need you. You are sacked.'

'Someone like you can't sack someone like me,' I said, 'sir.'

He thought for a second. 'Then resign. I will give you six months notice.'

Goenka sometimes kept his threats and promises. One of the *Express* editors was then put on to the task of attacking Antulay by alleging that he was corrupt, was mishandling the trusts and profiting from the sale of cement. Antulay was taken to court and his political career ruined. By this time I had ceased to be in Goenka's employment.

This came about by subtle stages. Goenka had at first pampered me like a favoured son. The ways in which I started to annoy him then multiplied. Antulay's refusal to supply him with cement enraged him; so did my constant inquiries as to when he proposed to start the promised magazine. I realized, later than I should have, that he had no intention of starting it at all. He had thought at the beginning that, as the biographer of Mrs Gandhi, I would have some pull with her, and with her government; that was why he employed me. When he found he had been mistaken, it angered him. He didn't like being mistaken. Our relations became more and more strained, till, at last, I resigned.

R.V. Pandit

My father said, 'Do you remember a man called R.V. Pandit? He came to see me the other day, and he was looking for you. He's gone back to Bombay now, but I think you should go there and talk to him. He says he has a job for you in Hong Kong. He says that it's very well-paid, and the sum he mentioned isn't unreasonable. He also says you'd have to travel a great deal in Asia.'

I remembered R.V. Pandit. He was one of those people whom one sometimes sees featured in the *Readers Digest* under some such title as 'The Most Unforgettable Man I Have Met'. I had first encountered him in 1959. He was slightly built, young, bespectacled, with a certain shyness about him. His most extraordinary attributes were his eyes, a pale, opaque green behind the lenses of his spectacles, with a perceptive look in them always. He was very intense, but could produce a charming, boyish smile and an unexpectedly high-pitched laugh.

What he did was mysterious, but he seemed to have a finger in many pies. Among other things, he occasionally helped my father, to whom he was a personal assistant, at least some of the time. My father asked him to assist me in Bombay, since I was not now familiar with the city. It had changed greatly during my three years abroad. Pandit and I became friends. His initials didn't seem to stand for anything. In fact, he was very secretive about them. He was simply called Pandit. He seemed to prefer it.

The whole city was his beat. Everyone knew him, and he had some mysterious friends. Once I had a colossal crapula after a party, and happened to meet him. I told him about it. 'What shall we do?' he asked. I replied that in London I would go to a pub and have a drink, and that would cure me. But in Bombay, with its prohibition laws, this was not possible. 'You only want to drink, hah?' said Pandit. 'Come with me.' He led me to the biggest and most expensive hotel in the city, and took me upstairs. Then he produced a key from his pocket, opened the door of a suite, and ushered me in. A well-furnished bar occupied a corner of the drawing room; he pointed to it. 'Help yourself,' he said, and I did. After a while someone turned the key in the suite's door, and came in. This person was a young Indonesian. 'Oh, it's you, Pandit,' he said. We were introduced. His name was Adrian Zecha, and he was a famous businessman in the Far East, though I didn't know this then. He seemed pleased that I was drinking his liquor, even if uninvited.

Afterwards, Pandit said, 'I have business dealings with him.' He did not elaborate.

These 'business dealings' sounded the more remarkable because Pandit was very poor. He lived in a small room above a Chinese restaurant in Colaba, and told me that he had lived in worse places. Otherwise, the aura of mystery that had commenced to collect around him deepened, at least in my mind.

I used to lecture in some of the city colleges, and at one lecture I noticed an African student sitting in an otherwise empty row. The rest of the hall was packed. None of the other students spoke to him.

Afterwards he came up to me. I asked him out for a cup of tea. Over it he told me bitterly that, though he had been a student in Bombay for two years, he was shunned by his Indian peers. No girl would dream of going out with him, and it was difficult to find lodgings. People in the street shouted 'Hubshee!' at him: the equivalent of 'nigger!' He could not wait to return to Kenya. The few other African students in town, his only friends, shared his desire to go home, because they had shared his experience. I was horrified. I asked, 'Have you *no* Indian friends at all?'

He said, 'Only one. He is called R.V. Pandit. Every Saturday he invites us all to tea in his room. He is the only one I can talk to.' It turned out to be true, though Pandit seemed shy to admit it. 'Poor fellows,' he said. 'In situations like these, I feel ashamed of my country.' I attended one of these teas. Pandit proved to be an excellent host. But, when I said the Africans must be very grateful, he blushed a bit.

'You know something?' he eventually said. 'Very few Africans, as yet, come abroad for their education. These boys are the sons of chiefs. Many of them will go from here to England and America for further studies. When they finish, they will go home. As more and more African nations become independent, they will have more and more power in their own countries. When I go there on business, they will remember me.'

All this was absolutely inexplicable. There were cases in India of poor men who had become rich. But these men had been ungentle and unscrupulous; Pandit was their opposite.

★

I remembered him when I returned to London, but was surprised when he telephoned me one day and said he was in town. I met him several times. He had put on weight, and looked somehow accustomed to money. He didn't, however, have very much. This, he explained, was because of the Indian controls on foreign exchange.

Once, towards the end of his stay, we were walking down Piccadilly, towards a pub, when it came on to rain. I had no raincoat. Pandit insisted that I should take his, a gesture in the tradition of Walter Raleigh, and I was deeply touched.

In the pub, we sat at a table and he said, 'Are you worried about something?'

I said I was. I do not usually confide in people, but I told him that I was very broke and had some bills to pay before my next cheque was expected. 'How much do you need?' he asked. I said I didn't want him to lend me money. 'Not me,' he said. 'I can't. But how much do you need?' I told him, 'About fifty pounds.' He nodded and said, 'Come with me.'

I was much reminded of the occasion in Bombay when he had found me a drink in the desert. We went into an office where a burly man with a moustache sat behind a desk. 'This is Gordon Landsborough,' Pandit said. 'He is a publisher. Gordon, he needs fifty pounds. Give it to him.' Landsborough was unruffled by this peremptory demand. He called his secretary, and she shortly brought in fifty pounds. It was the first time in my life that I had ever obtained hard cash from a publisher on request. But Pandit was completely unsurprised. 'Good,' he said, 'Thanks, hah, Gordon. Now I think we can leave.'

Pandit had now really become wealthy. He owned the magazine *Imprint* in India. He also owned a publishing house, and the most expensive bookshop in Bombay. He owned Indian restaurants in Monte Carlo and Nice. He lived in Hong Kong. When he came to Bombay, he had a permanent suite reserved for him at the hotel where Adrian Zecha had once stayed. I met him there. He was, as he had always been, dressed in a suit, but this one was of a more expensive material and cut than in the past. The drawing room was strewn with papers, files and magazines, and Pandit seemed to belong to it, to belong to a world of high finance and business transactions to which I was a complete stranger.

He explained his proposition to me rapidly, though not very concisely. He had, at some point in the last decade, started to work for the *Asia Magazine*, which then had offices in Singapore. It had been the brainchild of a Singapore Chinese, a multimillionaire called Norman Soong. He thought it up at about the time that the Sunday supplements were starting up in Britain. There were English papers all over Asia: none of them had Sunday supplements. Soong felt that a magazine could be published, its contents of general Asian interest, and inserted as a supplement into one paper in each Asian country, if the paper paid for it. The logistics were tremendous, but Soong and Adrian Zecha worked them out. At present, the *Asia Magazine*, now based in Hong Kong, had a readership of about six million. It went to eleven Asian countries, and had a board which comprised the heads of three of the papers it supplied, and also Rupert Murdoch. I told Pandit about meeting Gerry Delilkhan and Kishor Parekh in Kathmandu.

'Bah!' he said. 'They are no longer employed by me. The magazine was running at a loss. I promised the Board I would show a profit within two years. For this purpose I am employing three good men. One is Tom Dozier, who was the Latin-American editor for *Time/Life* for twenty years. He's very senior. He will be the managing editor. There will be two associate editors. One will be John Gale, from the *London Observor*. The other will be you. You understand?' He paused, breathless, though he had not yet had the sequence of heart-attacks that were later to make him more frenetic in his behaviour.

'Who else is there?' I inquired.

Pandit said, 'When I became the publisher, there were fifty or sixty people, all over Asia. Completely useless people. I sacked them all.'

I said in amazement and slight shock, 'All?'

'Well, nearly all,' said Pandit.

It wasn't quite as drastic as he had implied. He had kept on the secretarial staff, and the people in the art department. The accounts people also remained unchanged. Three of the former photographers remained in place, Henry Mok in Hong Kong, Takeshi Takahara in Tokyo and Dick Baldovino in Manila. He had also hired an Indian photographer, Ashvin Gatha, who was to be Hong Kong-based, and three young writers, who would also be in the Hong Kong office. 'They will take the load off your shoulders,' Pandit said. 'But first, since they know nothing, you will have to train them.'

'Is there any backlog left by the previous staff? I mean, have we got enough material to run a few issues still?'

'No,' said Pandit. 'Adrian Zecha has started a newspaper and a magazine. All these useless people went to him, and before they went they took all their material from the files. I am telling you, for the last few months I have run this magazine alone.'

The job looked harder and harder, the more I heard of it. But it also seemed a challenge; it could be exactly what I was looking for, since it entailed both a reasonable salary and constant travel; and I had no options. Next day I signed the contract, and Pandit flew back to Hong Kong, saying he would call me in a couple of weeks. Tickets would be sent for my wife Leela and myself. 'But you had better get married,' said Pandit, 'because in Hong Kong they are very strict about these things.' So we did.

★

Hong Kong island came up with the dawn, the mainland mountains behind it. I had never been this way before, and these mountains looked as though they had come out of a painted scroll. At the airport we were met by an Indian, Raj Gupta, who ran the Far East Trade Press, which Pandit owned and which put out trade magazines. He drove us through the Kowloon streets, packed with Chinese faces and the signs of bars and restaurants, and put us in the Hyatt. 'Tom Dozier has already come with his wife,' Gupta said. 'Tonight Pandit is throwing a party for him and for you.' I looked forward to this: I was eager for this new challenge in a new part of the world, and wanted badly to meet the people with whom I was to work. Leela and I spent most of the day asleep. At dusk, following Gupta's directions, we took a ferry across the harbour to Victoria, which is what the British authorities called the island, though nobody else did. The ride took twenty minutes.

I was often to take the ferry in the next two years. But the first impact was special. The island, a great hump across dark, flustered water, gleamed as with fallen stars, from the peak down to the illuminations of Wanchai: a turtle risen from the sea, spotted and streaked with phosphorescent weeds. We took a taxi to Pandit's flat. It was large and comfortable, and full of happily drunk people—Pandit's employees, Pandit's friends.

Two of them were Tom and Florence Dozier. Tom, who was to be my chief, was a lean, bespectacled man from the American south. He was in his middle years, and had had a great deal of experience with *Time/Life*. He spoke in a quiet drawl, interspersed with Santa Claus-like chuckles, ho-ho-hos, but in a very low key. He had been reading my autobiography. The office is a real mess,' he said, 'Pandit's been running it with three kids and Ted Gowing. Gowing's on loan from the Far East Trade Press, but he's a new arrival too. John Gale's coming in a couple of days, but Gowing's on loan to us till we settle.' He introduced me to Gowing's wife Jenny, a small, pretty, but slightly careworn blonde. They had a small baby, she said, and she was awfully worried about his health in a very foreign country. 'Of course,' she said, 'there's one consolation, he belongs to Britain.' At this moment her husband came up. He was lanky and blue-chinned, with a pleasant but rather undisciplined face, and was very drunk. 'I have been dancing with your wife,' he said. 'She has fantastic knockers.' I could see why Jenny looked careworn.

After the party was over, Pandit asked us to stay on. He looked rather careworn himself. I said so. 'I am worried,' he said; 'Did you see Ted Gowing tonight? He was *drunk*, I tell you. *Drunk*. And Dozier and you drink very heavily. It means that all three of you are alcoholics. My God! I have hired three alcoholics!' I interposed the stupidly defensive remark that neither Dozier nor I had been drunk, but he did not seem to hear, and continued, 'Do you know John Gale?' Not personally, I replied, but he was a good writer. 'Yes,' said Pandit with a sigh that seemed born of despair. 'He has written books. He has written an autobiography called, *Clean Young Englishman.* Have you read it?'

'No.'

'In it,' said Pandit, in a kind of wail, 'he confesses that he spent some time as a patient in a lunatic asylum. I do not know. It seems I have hired three alcoholics and a certified madman. What will the board say? What will Rupert Murdoch say? I do not know.'

Next day I turned up at the office. Leela went to an estate agent to find us a flat. The office was on the tenth floor of a building in Queen's Road, the main traffic artery of the island. The crowded street was alive with noise and people, rickshaws, cars, buses, trams, lorries. But the office was soundproof, a glass-encased haven, and very spacious. Chinese secretaries sat at tidy desks, the equipment was professional, and Pandit, Dozier and Gowing were there. I was allotted a room, and introduced to the rest of the staff. The three juniors were present. Jim Burke was a young American who had served in Vietnam. His father, also Jim Burke, had been an excellent photographer with *Life,* and had died falling off a Himalayan peak. Tom Dozier and I had known the elder Burke and his widow, Josephine. We, therefore, had an avuncular interest in Jim.

Erika Petigura was a tall, shy girl whose father was Indian. Her mother was Chinese, and Erika spoke Cantonese fluently. The third recruit was a Hong Kong Chinese named Peter Ling, who was thin, bespectacled and inarticulate. Tom Dozier said, 'We're supposed to train these kids. You take Peter, I'll take Erika, and John Gale can have young Jim.' We began to talk, to organize ourselves. Pandit, looking on, seemed to have overcome his fears of the previous night, and could even be said to look happy.

The following day John Gale arrived, and with him Pandit's fears returned. Shortly before Gale's plane was due, he came to my room and asked me to accompany him to the airport, 'Because,' he said, 'porters are hard to find at Kai Tak, and someone must carry his luggage.' Greatly affronted, I suggested he take Ted Gowing, who was younger and fitter than I was. He did. When Ted came back to the office, he was laughing uncontrollably.

'I've never seen anything like it,' he said. 'On the way to the airport Pandit told me that he thought Tom, you and I were all alcoholics. I must say I was a bit annoyed. Then he said that Gale had admitted in some book or other that he was a certified lunatic. He seemed a bit upset. He got more upset when Gale came off the plane with a carton of champagne under each arm. He turned pale. He said, "This one is so desperate for alcohol that he carries it with him on the plane! I tell you, Gowing, this is too much! Now I find that I have employed four alcoholics, and one of them is also a madman!"'

Gale, a large, flushed, robust man with a hearty manner, was much puzzled by all the fuss. 'I've been finishing a book on Africa,' he told us, 'and the night I left we had a party at home. When I left the house for Heathrow I thought the simplest thing was to put my notes and manuscripts in two empty champagne cartons. I carried them with me for safety. What's the matter with Pandit? He seemed frightfully upset. I don't understand him.'

'I don't think he understands any of us,' said Tom Dozier drily.

★

It was hard work at the office. The sacked staff had left nothing behind, no material we could use, not even photographs. The size of the magazine, between the time they had left and the time we arrived, had shrunk from forty-eight pages to sixteen. Desperate for material, Pandit had sent Jim Burke and the Indian photographer, Ashvin Gatha, who also took along his fiancée, Flora, to Malaysia. They had now come back. Gatha who had curly black hair down to his shoulders and dressed in designer denims and spectacular shirts, had not got on with Jim, a conservative in everything, but particularly in the matter of dress. Nor had the presence of Flora helped. All these factors had contributed to a futile trip.

★

At the office, John Gale refused absolutely to try and train anyone. This meant that I took charge not only of Peter Ling but of Jim Burke. As we scoured the Hong Kong landscape for fillers, I suggested to Jim that he keep an eye open for unusual stories. I had to explain what I meant by this. In a day or two he came back with one which suited me perfectly. This was about two topless waitresses who worked in a Wanchai club of his acquaintance. These two had been abandoned by their husbands—both were English—and supported themselves with their bosoms. But between them they had eight children, who lived with them in a flat they shared. I sent Jim after them to finish the story.

He presented it to me. The first three-quarters of it was an accurate, even rather witty, account of the dual lives led by the two women, as topless waitresses and fond mothers. But in the final bit Jim's innate conservatism took over. I couldn't imagine where he got it from—neither of his parents had suffered from this attitude. In his concluding paragraphs he unexpectedly turned on the hapless waitresses, called them women of low morals, and said they were unfit to be in charge of children. All that he had previously stated seemed to contradict this entirely. I chided him gently about this, and cut it.

I had intended to run two colour photographs with the article. One was to show the two ladies topless. The other was to show them fully dressed, plying their offspring with breakfast. Jim's fit of morality lasted long enough for him to tell the arts department, purely of his own accord, to airbrush the nipples out of the topless picture. A black wash was put over the two pairs of breasts, but, being transparent, lent a singularly suggestive air to the photograph. The *Manila Times* telexed us saying that the Philippines was a Catholic country. The Singapore *Straits Times* said that Lee Kuan Yew, the prime minister, had personally expressed his displeasure at the immorality of it all. Pandit blamed it on me. Jim failed to see that he had made a mistake.

In the meantime, Tom, the two Johns, and I produced our first issue. It was packed with fillers, but our own. We took great pride in it. The system was that the material was laid out and set in Hong Kong; every Saturday afternoon, two weeks before the actual publication date, we flew the sheets out from Kai Tak to Tokyo. Here it was printed and flown out to the eleven newspapers which took us. This first issue was pasted up and ready to leave on our first Saturday. An hour was left before the Tokyo flight took off. The messenger was waiting for us to hand the sheets over before he took the helicopter to Kai Tak. Pandit came in as we were about to do so. 'Let me see,' he said.

We unsealed and unwrapped the parcel. The lead piece was by me, about the relationship between mainland China and Hong Kong. It contained the sentence, 'Every day 20,000 head of cattle pass over the Shumchun bridge into the crown colony.' The sentence stays in my memory because Pandit, upon seeing it, screamed, 'Grammar! Grammar!'

We looked at him, wholly mystified. Seizing a blue pencil, he began to correct the paste-up. 'I thought your grammar was good,' he shouted. 'I will not have grammatical errors in my magazine! You say, "20,000 head of cattle." How can 20,000 cattle only have one head? It is heads—heads—heads!' The first thing we had to do was to convince him of his mistake. The second was to have a recorrection of the correction printed and repasted. Finally we were able to send the messenger to Kai Tak. He managed to put our package on the Tokyo flight. 'Are there going to be lots of bits like this?' John Gale asked innocently, when it was all over. Tom opened the office bottle, silent.

★

Pandit was one of the puzzles of life. I liked him very much, I was even fond of him, but he seemed a completely different man from the one I had met in Bombay a decade before. He had then been relatively simple, but was now complex, a bundle of sensitivities, chips that he mentally computerized borne heavily on his shoulder. He still had flashes of almost overwhelming generosity and kindness, but he always seemed to think that he knew best, about almost everything, which is a dangerous thing in a man. 'What's his first name?' John once asked me. 'He says call him Pandit, but then I sound like some kind of Hindu devotee.' Tom was puzzled too, which made three of us. 'He says he's interested in backing a Hindu political party in India.' Tom said, 'But I've also seen him praying in church on Sunday.' Tom and Florence were both devout Roman Catholics.

Some of the problems were resolved when, quite early on in our editorships, an ecumenical council was held in Hong Kong. One of the prelates who attended it was the Cardinal of Bombay, Valerian Gracias, who had been a great friend of my father's when they were both young. Since then, despite my father's views on religion, they had remained on amicable terms. At his and my mother's insistence, my father had had me christened, baptized and confirmed in the Catholic faith by him. Though perfectly aware I wasn't a believer, he was by way of being a friend of mine. He liked good Scotch.

When he came from India, we threw a party for him, to which I invited Pandit and my colleagues. Tom Dozier was delighted, Pandit unaccountably shy. I also ordered a large supply of good whisky. The Cardinal arrived in full regalia. After dinner, replete with food and drink, he allowed his eye to stray around the company. Presently it fell on Pandit, and he said, 'Who is this again?' I introduced them afresh. 'But I knew I recognized him,' said the Cardinal. 'His name is not Pandit. His name is Tommy Rodrigues, and, when I had my first parish in Bassein, he was a little barefoot boy who used to bring me bunches of bananas from his parents. Eh, Tommy? In those days your parents could not afford to buy you shoes, my son!'

Pandit was not only slightly embarrassed, but rather pleased. Indeed, he admitted, he was the very Tommy Rodrigues whom the Cardinal so fondly remembered. The mystery of his past had been cleared up, and he seemed relieved. For the rest of the party he conversed in whispers with the Cardinal, who, as a parting shot, blessed him with holy water. A couple of days later, John said to me in the Savoy, 'He was awfully chuffed, Pandit, wasn't he, to be blessed by the Cardinal? Afterwards he explained the whole thing to me. His family were high-caste Brahmins; that's why he calls himself Pandit. When the Portuguese occupied Bassein, wherever that is, they threw beefsteaks into the family well to pollute it. So the family lost its caste and became Catholics. That's why he's called Thomas Rodrigues. I'd have thought the Portuguese would have had more sense, wouldn't you, than to waste perfectly good beefsteaks by throwing them down wells? But there it is. Do you think,' asked John with a huge smile, 'now that all is known, he'd mind if I called him Tommy?'

II

Inherited Remains

Indira Gandhi

I first met Mrs Gandhi in December 1968 in highly inauspicious circumstances. At that time I had not visited the country of my birth for nine years: London was my home. Though I knew very little about India, when a Fleet Street editor wanted something about it without the trouble and expense of sending a correspondent there, or when a television producer needed someone to pontificate about the woes of the subcontinent, they asked me. Young and impecunious, I could hardly decline these offers, and wrote and talked on every topic remotely connected with the country, from Jawaharlal Nehru to tandoori chicken. In 1967 an editor asked me to write about Mrs Gandhi on the occasion of her fiftieth birthday. She had become, a few months before this, in 1966, the second woman in history to be prime minister of an entire country. Now I did know that she was Nehru's daughter, but that was about all I knew of her, for I was not in those days much interested in politics, especially not in the politics of a country seven thousand miles of sea, desert and mountains away from the British Isles. Nevertheless I accepted the assignment and read the office file on her. It consisted largely of critical articles: indeed, very critical articles. I concluded that she was a monster. As I said, I was less responsible then than I am, I hope, now, and I did a reasonably skilful piece which poked fun at her doings, though I did not know exactly what they were.

But when in 1968 I arrived in India, with the intention of writing a book (it never materialized) on the country, I realized it was necessary for me to interview the lady. I was staying with my father in Delhi, and, since he could arrange most things, I asked him to arrange this. He was uncharacteristically nervous about it. 'You see,' he said in his usual indistinct murmur, 'when you published that stupid article, parts of it were quoted here. Somebody asked her what she thought about it, and all she would say is that you were a very immature young man. I don't know if... but she's a mature person.' Using the phrase by which we affectionately called each other, he said, 'You stupid old fool, I'll try. But what do you want to ask her?' Having no knowledge of Indian politics, I could not say.

Despite all these difficulties, the interview was fixed. I saw her in her office. She was tiny behind an enormous desk, the white streak already in her hair seeming to be carved through the black of it. Her hooded eyes seldom looked at me, but over me at a photograph of her father that hung on the wall opposite her. She answered my questions more or less monosyllabically. She never smiled. Indeed, she appeared to become very tired of the whole interview about sixty seconds after it began. In these somewhat galling circumstances, I laboured on: the only time I got any real response was when I inquired if her father had had a tremendous influence on her in terms of the policies she adopted (what these policies were, in fact, I did not know). She looked at me for the first and only time during this ill-fated interview, frightening me with her eyes, and said, 'Does everyone who interviews me have to ask the same question?' I hastily switched to something else, and she returned to murmured monosyllables, occasionally looking rather pointedly at her watch.

I hung on doggedly until an aide entered and whispered something to her. A look of some relief came to her face and she nodded to the aide, who said, 'Madamji has another appointment.' I rose, wanly folded my hands to her in farewell, and trailed out in the wake of the aide.

One reason for my disappointment at this meeting was that during the course of it I found myself liking her. It is very difficult to say why one starts to like anybody. The sexual relationship between casual lovers, or husband and wife, seems to me usually to be a fusion, magnetic almost, of opposite poles: love, liking may come into it, but the actual liking of a person with whom you are not physically involved is different. You normally start to like somebody because you see resemblances between yourself and the other person. I had suddenly perceived, in the lady, that she and I resembled each other in a way: both with an inbred shyness born out of tumultuous childhoods; both with a certain dislike of too much talk and loquacious people; both, at our different ages, with a total tiredness of, and a total interest in, this burning and turning world. What upset me after the interview was not the fact that I had liked her and she had not liked me: she had given no real indication of dislike; it was the fact that I had liked her and I had been of no interest to her; she had done what was expected of her and then shelved me in her memory; the whole thing was over.

Though I saw resemblances between us even then, I did not and, of course, do not, ever expect to be seated behind a huge desk running a huge country. What I became interested in was how she came to be seated behind such a desk, how she came to run such a country.

★

Shortly after Mrs Gandhi was defeated, in March 1977, in the Indian elections she had called after she ended her Emergency, my wife, Leela, and I went to see her in New Delhi, at 1 Safdarjang Road, the house where she had stayed since she first became prime minister in 1966. She was supposed to move from it shortly, since her successor, Morarji Desai, who had a perfectly good house of his own in Dupleix Road, wanted to take 1 Safdarjang Road over as his official residence. It was a petty prod at Mrs Gandhi: but it must have hurt.

Mrs Gandhi sat in a large chair, her feet curled up under her. 'Thank you for coming,' she said. 'I'm sorry the house is so disorganized, but I'm supposed to move soon.' She looked terrible, worse than I had ever seen her even when as prime minister she followed her father's habit of working eighteen hours a day. Then the pouches under her sharp eyes had been those normally caused by tiredness and lack of sleep: now they were something else, they were black pouches, and she seemed physically to have shrunk. She was also, though very quiet as usual, not as watchful as usual, not as alert or as wary. She repeated, 'Thank you for coming,' and to my horror Leela burst into tears. Mrs Gandhi, courteous by nature, affected to be unaware of this, turned her tired eyes to me, and said, 'We've all the furniture and things to move, and we don't have a lot of time.' Leela, having somewhat recomposed herself, said, 'If I could help you pack...' and Mrs Gandhi blinked, smiled, sneezed like a little cat, and said, 'No, no, Leela, don't worry. Don't worry so much. I'm all right.' I then said, 'You look awfully tired.' To this, unblinking, but her hands curled in her lap, she replied, 'I'm better than I have been for a very long time. I feel as though an enormous weight has been lifted off my shoulders. Do you understand what I mean?' She later said this, perhaps less spontaneously, to several other people, including David Frost.

There was then a considerable silence, during which Leela dried her eyes and Mrs Gandhi and I stared past each other into the middle distance. Finally she said, 'I had lost touch with the people. Halfway through the election I felt here,' and with a typically unemphatic movement of her hand touched her chest, 'that we would lose. Well, we've lost.' There seemed little more to say. At length Mrs Gandhi said, 'They're setting up all these tribunals and commissions, so I suppose I'll have to face those.' With some asperity she added, 'I don't know why they want to waste so much money.' This was one of those conversations which proceed by stops and starts. 'Are you going to go back into politics, ma'am?' I asked. She said 'No. I told you I feel as though a burden has been lifted from my shoulders. I will never return to politics.' At that moment I didn't doubt what she had said.

A few days later I revisited her at Safdarjang Road, this time alone. Apart from her small grandchildren, the son and daughter of Rajiv, her elder son, and his Italian wife, Sonia, and a large and stately wolfhound, she was also alone. Moreover, even the furniture of the house, solid and palpable entities which can act as company to a lonely person, had vanished, or most of it had: it was being packed for transfer to 12 Willingdon Crescent, where she was now to live. This house had formerly been the home of Mohammed Yunus, an old family friend and at one time the special envoy of Mrs Gandhi. He had given it up so that her family could inhabit it.

So, amidst an absence of furniture and pictures, she sat, smiling only when the high voices of the children carried into the desolate house. It was the first time I had seen her with no aide or secretary hovering about. Even the telephone seemed dead: its bird-like cries, which had so often interrupted our conversations in the past, stilled, its chilled body lying black on the table.

I had come to broach a topic that I had raised on our last visit. In 1971 an American publisher had approached me, asking me to write a biography on what he called 'the most powerful woman in the world', Mrs Gandhi. The firm had approached Mrs Gandhi and she had expressed herself to be willing to cooperate. But at that time I was the editor of a magazine in Hong Kong, and I had a responsibility to it. I couldn't, therefore, write the book: anyway, I did not feel very strongly about the idea of a biography of a politician in power: an article, yes, a book, no. Somebody else wrote the book: 'I gave him,' Mrs Gandhi said with a faint smile, 'fifteen minutes of my time.'

I now thought, possibly, that Mrs Gandhi out of power would be far more interesting for me to write about than Mrs Gandhi in power. When I had asked her, at our previous meeting, if she would *like* me to write such a book, she had replied, 'Why not? If it wasn't you it would be someone else,' not a surpassingly modest remark. Today I said, 'Ma'am, do you really want me to write this book about you? I'd like to.' She shrugged a little. 'Then,' I said, 'you'll have to help me. I shall have to have much more of your time than fifteen minutes. Are you willing to spare me quite a lot of time?' She said, 'From now on I shall have a lot of time on my hands. Why not? Phone me next week, when we have moved.' I patted the children on the head, smiled weakly at the wolfhound, and left, thinking that this should not be a difficult book to write. Little did I know.

★

If you write about someone, you need to keep the person concerned under your eye, and you need to have kept them there for some time

I called on Mrs Gandhi one afternoon to clarify a couple of points. Outside the house in the roadway loitered a number of men trying so desperately to look normal that they were obviously from the Central Bureau of Intelligence. At the gate was a sort of red-brick pillbox from which Mrs Gandhi's own people checked prospective visitors. They knew me and waved me by. There is a short horseshoe drive in front of the house, surrounded by lawns dotted with flowerbeds and trees. The grass had started to brown and the flowers to wilt, for it was March, and the heat had begun to crawl into the city.

On the tired turf stood tents furnished with chairs, where Mrs Gandhi met her supporters. There were not many around today: it was hot, bees murmured stickily above the flowers, and such supporters as there were slept in the shadows of the tents, waiting for Mrs Gandhi to come forth in the cool of the evening. It was a good time for me to have come: the tents and lawns were usually full of raucous Congress workers.

The house itself has only one storey and rambles away to more lawns at the back, where a variety of tropical birds imitate the more discordant sounds of the Congress workers. There is a balcony in front, off which Mrs Gandhi's reception room opens, as well as a corridor that leads into the main body of the house. Here not only Mrs Gandhi but her two sons and their families live. A huge bamboo screen shields the front of the house from the dusty road, for 12, Willingdon Crescent had now become a milestone on the tripper route: tourist buses drew up outside, and inquisitive eyes and cameras peered around for the small, famous figure in its pastel saree, once ruler of the very dust churned up by these buses.

One of the Irish wolfhounds (there are five in the house, each the size of a large donkey) shambled out of the corridor and sniffed at me with the bored air of a sensualist in smells who finds nothing to detain his interest. Simultaneously, Mrs Gandhi popped her head out of the door of the reception room, smiled, and said, 'Come in.'

I followed her in. I had some flowers in my hand: she loves flowers, or rather, as she once said to me, she loves arranging flowers rather than the flowers themselves, a remark I think perhaps psychologically significant. She did not say anything as I handed them to her: it had now become a ritual between us, so that I did not need to say anything either. However, her right eyelid flickered in rapid succession several times, a facial mannerism that may mean irritation or pleasure, and she hurried off with the flowers to put them in water. The whole atmosphere surrounding my arrival was familiar to me now, the ritual like the formal steps of a dance. The reception room is small but comfortable with a sofa and several armchairs, and now came the final step of the dance: Mrs Gandhi entered and seated herself in the armchair to the right of the sofa, and I seated myself on the sofa to her left. This is our normal spatial relationship in this particular room: perhaps Robert Ardrecy would understand. As usual, Mrs Gandhi started off by saying nothing whatever.

Presently I inquired about her entry into politics. Why, I asked, had her father proposed to the Congress in 1959 that she should be president? Was this indicative of a desire that she should succeed him? The faulty mirrors of history: Mrs Gandhi stared at me, then said, 'I was *bullied* into the Congress presidency, you know. I didn't want it at all.' But, I inquired, had her father not taken her wishes into account? 'He was against it too,' she said. Everyone I had spoken to or read had conveyed an exactly opposite impression. She had not felt qualified for the post she said: she had felt shy, and she had wanted to look after her family. Her father had not wanted to seem to be pushing his only child into power.

The initial dust of summer floated in through the open door, and for the first time in months the wind that rustled the curtains was warm. Mrs Gandhi, with an irritable click of the tongue, closed the door and turned on the fan. Looking at her abstractedly, I had a strange sense that I was not in the room at all, but an observer peering down a telescope from some chilly star. To see an ordinary woman suddenly do something extraordinary: move across the room say, with the beauty of a ballerina, and, completely unconscious of that completed movement, sit down once more and talk of her servant problems, takes me aback. It took me aback far more to see an extraordinary woman suddenly doing something ordinary: pulling doors shut, drawing curtains to, flicking at switches to find the right one, then returning to her chair, the drawing of the saree across her shoulders like the reassumption of some mantle worn by right. I reflected that the woman who had shut the door was the one most people had seen and known until 1959. In 1959 she had suddenly, and against all expectations, proved that, firstly, she had ideas of her own, secondly, that her father had come to respect them, and thirdly, that she had acquired the drive to see her ideas carried out. Furthermore, I believe that 1959 was the first year in which she herself definitely realized that she *did* have ideas of her own. Miss Betty Friedan, an American writer, said that 'an unidentified source' told her 'that in the early days Nehru would bully Indira in an absolutely shocking way... shatter her self-confidence' and turn her 'into a mass of nerves'.

This account may or may not be true, but by 1959 Indira had developed confidence and not only the respect of her father but influence over him. Also, she had tasted power.

I looked at her. Somebody had fetched her a file. She had put on her spectacles and was frowning at it. She scribbled a note in the margin and turned back to me. I said, 'You really came into politics in 1959, didn't you, in an active sense?' One of her more enigmatic expressions came to her face then, as usual, was followed by a smile. 'If you like to think so,' she said. I pushed my question: she played with the hem of her saree in silence. I have noticed, though I cannot analyse the reason, that while she usually answers complex and difficult questions fluently, perfectly innocuous queries seem to drive her back into unplumbable depths of silence. Perhaps it is that a complex question is obviously a complex question, but that she is afraid that an uncomplex question may be a complex one wrapped up in wool. Finally I said, 'Okay, ma'am, we'll *assume* that the first active part you played in the politics of independent India was in 1959.' At this she laughed, and said, 'All right, *you* assume that.' I said, 'And you liked it.' She replied, 'I was needed.' Said in another way, it would have been a highly pretentious remark: but there was a kind of dual sadness in her voice, as though firstly, she was glad that someone *had* needed her, so that she could be of use, and secondly, as though the need for her that had started then had since pulled at her whole life hard enough to hurt. 'But,' I said, 'you refused to stand for a second term as Congress president in 1960. Weren't you needed then?' She looked a little irritated. 'My husband was ill,' she said. 'We were closest in his last years. My father was old, and my sons were young.'

'But between 1960 and 1965, you weren't much concerned in politics, were you?'

'Yes, I was.' It was a sudden irritable flash. 'I was in politics all the time. Let's be clear about it. I didn't hold any cabinet post or anything like that, but I was on the Congress Working Committees and on other committees. I watched it all... I watched them all.' I said, 'In 1962, when the Chinese attacked India and your father was heavily criticized, and abandoned by his supporters, did you develop a distrust of people which you have still?' She thought about this for a moment, right elbow on knee, right thumb pressed against her underlip. At this moment Sonia, the wife of her elder son Rajiv, entered with the flowers I had brought. Mrs Gandhi turned her attention from me to them. 'Put the pink ones in the vase here,' she said. 'I think we should break up the colours... and the red ones in the dining room. And the rest in my bedroom. Don't arrange them, I'll come and do that later.' Sonia smiled at me and went out with her dripping and fragrant burden, a wolfhound who looked as though its ancestor might have persecuted the Baskervilles at her heels. Mrs Gandhi turned to me again. 'Well,' she said, 'if you have heard that I've distrusted people since 1962, that isn't true at all. In fact, I don't distrust people, rather the opposite. I often think that my chief fault in life has been my trustfulness.'

★

The next time I phoned, Mrs Gandhi had completed her move.

I arrived, found crowds of people outside 12 Willingdon Crescent, which I hadn't previously visited, tentsful of people on the lawns, Congressmen on the verandah and, in the reception room with which I was to become increasingly familiar over the next year, two persons, one of whom was an old friend of my father's, G. Parthasarathi, known to his intimates as G.P., who had been an excellent cricketer and had nearly played for India. He had later become an outstanding diplomat, had been vice-chancellor of the Jawaharlal Nehru University in Delhi, and most recently, head of the Planning Commission. The other person, a short and affable person, was D.P. Singh, a famous lawyer. 'We,' said G.P., 'are protecting Mrs Gandhi's interests. On the matter of this book, we want to know what exactly you have in mind.' Being entirely unprepared for this, I stuttered somewhat. 'You see,' said Mr Singh in his affable way, 'the party may not like it if you print certain things she tells you.' I was surprised: 'I thought she wasn't in politics,' I said. 'What has any party to do with this?' Mr Singh shook his head. 'No, no,' he said patiently. 'Who has said she is not in politics? Who is to lead our party?'

These discussions lasted several weeks. Sometimes Mrs Gandhi was present, frowning a little and scribbling notes: sometimes it was only G.P., Mr Singh and myself. At one point, utterly mystified by what was happening, I flew to London to consult my agent. He was as mystified as I by the proceedings and shortly after I flew back to Delhi he came over to try and sort the matter out. He returned to London even more perplexed than before. There were, according to Mr Singh, certain aspects of Mrs Gandhi's life I could write about, certain aspects the party would not like me to write about, certain matters she would help me with, certain matters she would not be allowed by the party to help me with, and so on and so forth.

One day Mrs Gandhi asked me to come and see her, and when I did, she said, frowning, hands folded in her lap, 'I don't see what all this fuss is about. I'm not authorizing this biography, am I? As you see, I am now trying to help the country, in my own way.' What she meant, obviously, was that she was now back in politics.

'I won't have the time I thought I'd have,' she added, 'when we first talked about this book of yours. But I'll help you as much as I can. I can't promise you anything, but I'll try.' After so many deaths, as George Herbert said, I lived and wrote. But the extraordinary chain of circumstances that led up to my writing this book seem to me worthy of record, if only because they confirmed my view that in all the ground around her, advisers bulge up like mushrooms after rain, sometimes because she wants them, sometimes not, and that in the end she tends to disregard all the advice and to do exactly what she thinks or feels is most sensible.

At about this point, I asked Mrs Gandhi and her family to dinner. She came, and it was obviously a release for her, in the sense that nobody discussed politics, and Leela, who is partly French, cooked a French dinner, and everybody liked it. Next day, one of the leading papers published, in a front page box, a story which said that Mrs Gandhi had been asked to dinner by us, that she had demanded numerous French dishes, that I had been so unnerved by these requests that I had asked a French diplomat for the services of his chef, that at the last moment I received a demand from Mrs Gandhi that I should not serve a certain kind of pudding, and this had led to the total disorganization of the dinner. When I saw this item in the newspaper, I phoned Mrs Gandhi and said I would write a disclaimer, which I did. The editor would not publish it in full, but enough of it appeared to show that the original story had been a lie. Meanwhile, Mrs Gandhi, before she saw my disclaimer, wrote me a small, cold letter: I would not have believed that she thought I would have betrayed her with a lie but she, I knew, was accustomed to betrayal, though I was sorry to think she equated me with her political colleagues.

The difficulty, the delicacy, of dealing with such a person, so often hurt, so often betrayed, was compounded at the time by her alertness about everyone who surrounded her, her reluctance to be further hurt, further betrayed.

My acquaintance with Mrs Gandhi had by this time spread over a decade, and it had always been a friendly one. Since her defeat in the elections, as I have said before, it had turned into a relationship, at least on my part, of closeness and care. The questions I asked her were always answered a little evasively except when she was in a good mood. Sometimes, even when she was in a bad mood, she answered, if she thought the question of interest, cohesively and clearly. People tend to be cyclical in their behaviour: they have a night and a bright day. To me, she is a good and gentle woman who lost part of her heart on the way to wherever she now is.

People call her a liar. I would rather say she prevaricates, evading the definite statement in conversation, but, when she acts, she is not a liar to herself. She has been called ruthless, and she is: this is also because she trusts nobody. She saw her mother scorned by other members of the family: she saw her father betrayed by those in whom he placed his chief trust. She is something of an intellectual, but her lack of trust has led her to believe that the sword is mightier than the pen. She is a remarkable woman as it is, probably the most remarkable woman I have ever met: but she could have been equally remarkable as a completely different sort of woman, if her childhood, her adolescent loneliness, her broken marriage, and her long watch over the dying days of her father, could be replaced and made into one. The absence of trust, the frequency with which she has been betrayed, contribute to this. It has led to temporary dependence on bad advisers, sycophants who tell her what she wants to know, because she believes they tell her the truth. Even during the Emergency she believed those who told her how much the people loved Sanjay. It has also led her to suddenly throwing good advisers out, because they have told her the truth. Pilate had the right line written for him in the New Testament: truth is not an exactitude: it varies from person to person. Pilate was not being sardonic when he asked what truth was, and Mrs Gandhi does not ask what truth is, so long as it is what she, against all evidence, believes.

★

Some months before she won at Chikmagalur, on a hot dusty July afternoon, I received a telephone call from Mrs Gandhi's office, asking for my exact address, since Mrs Gandhi had written me a letter. This was not normal procedure: her officials knew my telephone number and my address already, and Mrs Gandhi did not usually write to me: she had someone telephone if she wanted to see me or speak to me. Our last meeting, a few days before, had been very friendly: but the peculiar circumstances, and the tone of the secretary on the telephone, made me feel that something important, indeed momentous, had happened in the few intervening days. I hate to wait for things to happen, so I said I would come and collect the letter. I drove round to Willingdon Crescent, where a usually smiling secretary nodded coldly at me and handed it over. Standing in the dusty sunlight on the lawn, I opened it and read it. The sand-wind made the letter shake in my hands, ribbing the fold with brown dust. I looked up from it at the balcony, where several secretaries were now apparently on sentry duty. I inquired if Mrs Gandhi was available, since I would like to speak to her. 'It is the afternoon,' they replied in a kind of Gregorian chant. 'She is asleep.' So I left.

I re-read the letter on the way back. It was polite and civilized, but too civilized, too polite: it was also very vague in its terms, and from my knowledge of Mrs Gandhi, such as it was, I interpreted it as a severance of relationship, especially since it did not require an answer. At first I experienced the kind of dull shock that many others must have done during their contact with Mrs Gandhi. Barely a week ago, my friendship for her and trust in her had been, apparently, mutual. Now, because of rumours of unspecified stories I had written about her, brought to her by unnamed people, this period was obviously over. I had started by wanting to be an eye that watched her and an ear that listened: I had ended by feeling strong sympathy for her as well as friendship, the two being not always inseparable: now the friendship had gone, drifted away on a wind of distrust, for all the good wishes she conveyed at the end of the letter.

When I started the book, I had asked her to read the chapters, since numerous interpretations of fact arose from the many interviews I had had with other people. I had said at the time that I wanted her corrections on facts, not of any opinions I might form during my research on those facts. 'It wouldn't be right for me to read a book written about me,' she said. That was all right by me.

Back home, I sat down and wrote her a letter. If she thought, I said, that I had misquoted her and perpetrated untruths, I was sorry. But since she had not read the book, nor had anyone in India except Leela, I wondered what her sources of information were.

A day later I telephoned one of the secretaries to ask if Mrs Gandhi had received the letter. 'Oh, yes,' he said, 'letter is at present in front of Madamji herself. She is reading it.' I inquired when I could see her. 'Oh, she wants to see you too much,' said the secretary, 'but do not worry yourself to call us, we will call you.'

I have said that after our trouble in 1978, I had not seen her, though I had followed her activities in the press. Leela and I sent her a Christmas card in 1978, and she sent us a

New Year card back with a friendly inscription. She must have been deeply depressed at the time, one of the worst periods of her life, and I thought it exceptionally kind of her. During much of 1979 I was in England, but towards the end of the year, considering all wounds healed, I took some flowers to Willingdon Crescent to wish her luck in the elections. She did not speak much, since we were surrounded by her followers, but she smiled. The atmosphere amidst her followers was one of some anxiety. The elections were due very shortly.

A few weeks later, on the day that her total victory was declared, I returned to Willingdon Crescent in the winter sunshine. It was crisp weather, with a wind flowing past me. The garden was packed with people, and there were hundreds outside the house. Drums thumped, bugles blared, flags clattered overhead. There were continual shouts of *'Indira Gandhi ki jai'* and *'Indira Gandhi, desh ka neta'*, cries I had heard before in very different situations. I struggled through the crowd to the front steps. For me they had numerous memories. I had come up them in all weathers, and I had seen Mrs Gandhi in this house in a variety of moods. Now the balcony was full of supporters, not all of whom had been supporters in the two years of her political exile.

Fortunately, one of her aides saw me. He took me by the arm and piloted me through the dense mass of bodies into the reception room, also full of people. Some sat, most stood. I stood, there being no more room to sit. At one point Sanjay appeared at the door, draped, like a young Caesar, in a purple shawl. He exchanged a few words with one of the Congressmen near the door, apparently to the effect that his mother would soon appear. Then he disappeared himself. The drums went on outside. Suddenly Mrs Gandhi, in a saree of pastel colours, framed herself in the doorway, slight and with a smile on her face. The Congressmen and women present folded their hands to her. When some had left, and there was more room, others knelt on the floor and touched her feet. I had heard her reprimanding people in the past for this habit, but today she did not, possibly because there were so many people and there was no time for lectures. Finally the room was empty except for her and me. She looked different from the way she had looked for two years: somehow taller.

Standing there, facing her, the echoes of the thousands of words we had exchanged in this room resounded in my ear. I recalled her sadnesses and silences, the brief time of her triumph when I had met her after her first arrest and release. 'Congratulations, ma'am,' I said. 'Could I—' The words 'see you sometime?' were cut short on my lips. 'Not now, Dom,' said Mrs Gandhi, 'I haven't *one* minute to spare.' She kilted up her saree and flew out of the front doorway. I watched her disappear into the sunshine and the cheering crowds.

On 14 January 1980, Mrs Indira Gandhi was sworn in for the fourth time as prime minister of India.

Jag Pravesh Chandra

We were in Delhi. It was 1997. The next day, 15 August, was the fiftieth anniversary of Indian independence. Everyone we met asked us the same question: 'What have we done in fifty years?' It was a dull, overcast day, slightly bloated by heat. I nodded at the driver, a muscular young Sikh in a pink turban. 'Hello, Sohan Singh.' The driver beamed. 'Where to, saheb?

'Khan Market,' I said.

I studied the city as it passed me by. The traffic oozed thickly and slowly down the broad, tree-lined thoroughfares. This was rich Delhi, the Delhi of foreign missions and five-star hotels, but the gridlocks here were as frequent as anywhere else. The morning was polluted, in different ways, by the reek of exhaust fumes and burnt rubber, the crow-like clamour of horns. Limp banners, stretched across the streets between bamboo poles, proclaimed the imminence of the fiftieth anniversary, and the billboards were adorned with patriotic pictures: Mahatma Gandhi, Nehru, even the present prime minister, I.K. Gujral. But the crowds of white-clad pedestrians and bicyclists, and the people in cars, almost all on their way to work, didn't seem in a festive mood.

As we approached Khan Market, Sohan Singh asked where exactly in Khan Market I wanted him to take me.

'70 Khan Market,' I told him, and the young man gaped. 'Saheb, that is Jag Pravesh Chandra's house.'

'Yes, I'm going to see him.'

Sohan Singh drove slowly, so as to be able to make enquiries. 'You are friend to Mr Jag Praveshji, saheb?' I said, 'Yes, he's an old friend.' Sohan Singh smiled. 'He help all Punjabi people in 1947, saheb, when they coming to this our Delhi with no money only. When my grandfather come as a refugee, Jag Pravesh help him. All my families is laarwing Jag Praveshji.'

Sohan Singh stopped at the mouth of a narrow bylane. Inside it was Jag Pravesh's house. His mother used to live with him, I recalled, but had died recently, at the age of 103. Before her death, or so Jag Pravesh had told me when we had last met, she had developed a new set of teeth, and her hair, scanty as I remembered it, had not only grown back but reverted to its former blackness.

He was now the leader of the Congress opposition in the Delhi assembly. A government car filled most of the entrance to his lane. It was a perquisite of his position, and came with a national flag and a dishevelled driver. I climbed a steep flight of stairs to a barsati. During the day, the household laundry was hung there to dry, as it was today. Around the barsati were small rooms: one of them was Jag Pravesh's office, where a Congress worker hammered at an ancient Remington typewriter. Jag Pravesh clearly didn't pamper his staff with computers.

Inside another small room, his bedroom and study, he awaited me, seated on his bed. The room, which was very crowded, also contained shelves heaped with files and pamphlets, and a cupboard in which he kept his few clothes and his liquor. He welcomed me, and immediately said, 'Come, let us go.' This phrase, which always seems comic to me, is very common all over India. 'Where?' I asked, but Jag Pravesh was already on his way out.

He was a small and wizened man, usually dressed, as he was today, in a safari suit. At eighty-three, he had a very spry air about him. Sohan Singh rushed up to touch his feet in homage. Jag Pravesh grimaced and remarked, 'We Indians are too servile.' He spoke to Sohan Singh in Punjabi. Sohan Singh smiled. 'I have asked about the health of his family,' said Jag Pravesh, 'and told him to follow my car.'

He got into his car. I joined him, and promptly bruised my elbow on a block of fossilized wood that lay on the seat. I had noticed over years that my friend's most inexplicable possessions always turned out handy. In this he was certainly Gandhian. Jag Pravesh placed the block of wood between us and used it as an armrest. It served its purpose admirably.

'I thought we were going to talk,' I protested, as the car started to move. He replied, 'Baba, we have been talking, off and on, for the last twenty-five years. Now I have to attend an Independence celebration for schoolchildren. I am the guest of honour and I am already forty minutes late. No matter, my dear, no matter. They cannot start the proceedings till I am there.'

'You are surprised to see me in such good health,' he said, as car horns brayed all around. 'But I am a fortunate man. My mother watches over me all the while.' He glanced at my expression and added hastily, 'Yes, I know she has passed away. But soon after her death, when I was occupied in the toilet, I clearly heard her voice. It said, "Child, child, you must quickly get out from this toilet." As I moved away, a huge stone fell from the roof on the place where I had been. Had I stayed there, I would have been killed.'

He added with relish, 'The fall of the stone made such a noise that people thought I had been assassinated by a bomb explosion, and the police came. A Madrasi fellow is the in-charge for the maintenance of the house. He is employed by the government. I told him my mother saved me. He said, "Saheb, if a big Congress leader like you died by my negligence, I would be thrown out from my position. So I must offer some gift in the temple to your mother, though she has passed away. By saving your life she has also saved my career."'

'So you have come to see us celebrate the fiftieth year of Independence. This year the celebrations will be a farce,' said Jag Pravesh. 'What is there for us to celebrate? I was there in 1947 when Panditji said at midnight that we were keeping a tryst with destiny. What bloody tryst, baba? As yet we have missed the tryst.'

His driver turned off the modern highway into a congeries of stunted and often unpaved alleys, and stopped. The alley lay beyond, full of small shops, and several policemen stood around. They saluted Jag Pravesh. A blare of patriotic music emanated from somewhere very close. It grew in volume as I followed him down the alley, which was caked with moist fritters of animal and human excrement, and refuse of various kinds. The heavy air held a stench of decayed vegetable matter. I kept my eyes down, careful where I walked.

Jag Pravesh said, 'Look at this! They say that Indians have no civic sense because it is a new concept in India. But I tell you, for fifty years now we have been trying to drum civic sense into the people. It is not new, it is only that they don't accept it.' He was very angry. 'This is a Congress meeting,' he said. 'Our party workers should have cleaned up this area. Where is our discipline? It is shameful.'

A crowd choked the throat of the alley. Several police officers were there too. They cleared a path, not very gently. I found myself in an open compound where khadi-clad Congressmen sat on a wooden platform, islanded in a sea of red-and-white school uniforms. Jag Pravesh grasped my arm like a cousin of the Ancient Mariner, and wouldn't let go. We were both pushed and hauled onstage. A gramophone with a horn, which I thought must have considerable antique value, stood on a table. The patriotic sounds that came from it deafened me, and I lowered my head to look down at two hundred children, who gaped back.

They were equally distributed as to gender and their

upturned faces, though young, were by no means innocent. They seemed recently to have been fed. On the ground around us, and sometimes still clutched in their hands, were paper packets that had contained food, and any casual observer could see what food it had been: chapatis, vegetable curry, daal, a sweetmeat. The thick yellow daal didn't seem to have been popular—trodden puddles of it smeared the floor of the compound, as though several drunks had vomited there. The puddles were swarmed over by plump black flies. Somebody thoughtfully stopped the gramophone.

A microphone came into use instead, and one by one everyone on the platform, except Jag Pravesh, rose and bellowed into it. I could recognize the names of Gandhi and Nehru, frequently uttered; and, less frequently, that of I.K. Gujral. The flies that had fattened on the discarded daal now hummed indolently through the air. My shirt was sodden and unbelievable quantities of sweat trickled down my face and neck. The flies, having fed, had descended on me to drink. Jag Pravesh, I noticed with awe, did not sweat at all. Perhaps it had to do with his age.

Contradicting this theory, the children didn't sweat either. But they had become restive, and now and then teachers, in Western shirts and trousers, or in sarees, went among them and swatted the less quiescent on the head with their hands or with wooden rulers. Several alleys led into the compound, and each was now filled with adult spectators: local residents? Parents? Both? And policemen. In addition to the Congressmen on the microphone, film music could be heard from the radios of the houses around. I started to feel that this would never end.

Then Jag Pravesh pulled at my sleeve. We descended from the platform, not without difficulty. The policemen once more cleared a way, and we came back to the cars. Jag Pravesh settled down comfortably, elbow on his fossil armrest, and said, 'Now we can take some coffee.' I said I had to pick someone up.

Before I got back into Sohan Singh's car, we made another date.

'You may think I have wasted your time,' Jag Pravesh said, through his window. 'But I wanted you to see this. It's very important that these children learn about our history. They are not taught properly in school. Now that the fiftieth anniversary is here, we have these meetings all over the city. After all, the Congress won the freedom struggle, not the BJP or any other party. They should be told that.'

I said, 'So it's all political really?' Jag Pravesh chuckled hoarsely. 'Tell me, my dear, what in India is not political? We even have to politicize our patriotism. But, seriously, these rallies do some good. The children are told to revere the motherland, to respect all religions, and not to do bad deeds. As adults, we can feel hope when we tell them to do whatever we have failed to do ourselves.'

On the way back to the hotel, I wondered why Jag Pravesh came into my mind whenever I thought of India. The gigantic partition of the subcontinent, the partition within it of flesh from flesh, damaged it internally: irreparably, and forever. Independence, after this, had been a voyage undertaken for its health, to help it recuperate. It had had the opposite effect in the end, but Jag Pravesh was one of those able and dedicated people who had stayed at the bedside from the start. He was like Whitman's sea captain: he could say without falsity, 'I am the man; I suffered; I was there.' He had worked for his party according to its original tenets. He had worked for the people. His own small tragedy had been the result of India's catastrophe. It had overlooked his services. He was never called upon to be a minister. He did not greatly mind; he was still there, waiting to serve, but now too old.

The remarkable fact about him was that he was still interested in the future of India. He was fairly cynical, and another person would have surrendered years ago to bribes or to hopelessness. But his cynicism, tolerant, accepted that most people in India had a price, and were capable of almost any action that was personally profitable. He had chosen not to be like that. I thought of him as unique, but it seemed probable that there had been others like him during the Independence movement and the early years of Nehru. If they had had any power over the nation, it might not have fallen into decline. They chose to stay in local politics because they were most effective at that level. They might have been as effective higher up; but nobody asked them, perhaps because they could not have been manipulated.

But another point about Jag Pravesh, simultaneously his strength and his weakness, was that he knew little of the world beyond India, its opinions, or its values. His own were those of a well-born North Indian, though liberalized because the Congress, once, was socialist. He had never travelled outside India, nor evinced any desire to do so. But he was convinced that no foreigner could understand India, and that nobody could who had not been brought up in a traditional Indian way, and who did not think like an Indian. What he meant by Indian did not exclude Muslims or other minorities, but it excluded me. He felt affectionate towards me, but amused: exactly the way I did, the other way round.

Mrs Ali, Wali Aasi and Nasser

The morning was hot and ominously low black clouds gathered over Lucknow. The landscape was emerald after rain, but wore a battered look. I showered, changed, and looked at the local paper. The front page said that a well known and badly wanted gangster had been seen in the city the previous evening. He had been speeding in a white Toyota car, and a police patrol had stopped him. The policemen recognized the driver, but had been too terrified to arrest him.

Nasser Abed, a senior journalist whom I knew, and who had lived in the city all his life, was to meet us. He arrived. We drove to a congested market area to buy liquor. Sarayu narrowly escaped being run over by a bullock cart. We drove to La Martiniere, Nasser's old school, and also, according to Kipling, Kim's. We drove to the old British Residency, made famous after the Mutiny of 1857. It was surrounded by gardens through which we walked, in spite of the sullen heat and the threat of rain. By the time we returned to the hotel, I had begun to be friends with Nasser. I poured drinks, and then the phone rang. The hotel manager wanted to welcome us. Could we come down and have coffee with him, or a drink? We went down and had a drink in the coffee shop, at one end of the main lobby. The manager was a slim young man from Delhi. 'It's difficult to adapt to Lucknow,' he said. 'I was here when the hotel was being built. Armed men used to drive up and demand protection money. Once it was built, it was hard to keep gangsters out, but we managed. It's perfectly safe inside the hotel. Our security is excellent.

'But my family and I live some distance away. The facilities there are fine. We even found a ballet school for our little girl. But one hears of kidnappings, wives and children held for ransom. I'm a little nervous to leave my wife and the little one at home, and sometimes when I'm delayed here and go home very late, I'm nervous about my own safety.'

★

Next day we lunched at the market, off a mutton biryani. Nasser said, 'I'm trying to fix an appointment for you with Mayawati, but so far no luck. So I've arranged for you to meet a Muslim politician, a lady, Mrs Ali. She's with the Congress. She has a rich husband.'

The ancient city seemed to be composed of several different villages with no relationship with one another. The area where the Alis lived contained modern houses and was like the residential areas in other Indian towns, but nothing like any other part of Lucknow I had so far seen. Mr Ali received us in a room that contained modern furniture and antique pieces that went together surprisingly well.

'It is the population,' said Mr Ali. 'That causes the trouble.' We had by now been comfortably arranged in well-upholstered chairs, and provided with sharbat. 'In our time,' he was in his late forties perhaps, and it was hard to tell what he meant, 'this was a very pleasant city, with a population of two or three hundred thousand. But now it is two million and there is chaos. That is an explosion. Isn't that an explosion? It started in the 1950s. We can't find places to park, our children find it difficult to get into schools, all because of overpopulation.' He seemed very excited.

'Sanjay Gandhi, he had the guts to force the people to accept birth control. But because of his firmness in the matter,

Mrs Gandhi lost the whole of North India in the 1977 elections. But what else was Sanjay to do? So many eminent people foretold this population explosion but nobody had the guts to stop it except him. People were saying that his policies were undemocratic. Why should he have cared for democracy?'

I enquired whether Mr Ali felt democracy was suitable to the Indian situation. He shook his head violently. 'I feel it is not. Here democracy is another name for indiscipline. They have exploited freedom and filled the political parties with criminals. Nobody does anything to stop it. Even the Congress gave tickets to gang leaders in Gorakhpur and here in Lucknow. The BJP did the same. Nobody cares for other people's rights. Even generally, the way our political parties generate money, the way the bureaucracy can amass wealth through corrupt methods, it is alarming.

'Many bureaucrats have become millionaires. It is shocking. If you go to a government office to get your work done, nothing will be done unless you pay heavy bribes. I'm a chemical engineer and in my work I have to get government permits very often. So I know, I know.'

Mrs Ali had not appeared. Her absence had so far been left unexplained, but her husband, as though he had read my mind, said, 'She will come.' This was said almost as an aside, and he plunged back into his monologue. 'Once people were saying the British should come back, but they won't say it now. And why should we want them back? For us it was a humiliation that they were here. They did good work but they did it for themselves. They only built railways and roads as supply lines for their troops. I don't know what British rule was like but I am told that the British were just, fair and very punctual. Everyone says they were very punctual. But they exploited us economically.'

He had a heavy and serious face, like a bloodhound. 'You want to interview my wife. She will come soon. That other fellow, what was his name, Naipaul, he also interviewed her.

She will come. Listen, I have visited Singapore. That is a small place, but so neat and clean. People there have a high standard of living. They have taken to modern ways of life, they are always most punctual. We should try to be like that. They had this benevolent dictator, this fellow, Lee Kuan Yew. We should also have a benevolent dictator. The Singapore people obeyed this Lee Kuan Yew; they keep the law.

'Here people have lost all respect for the law. On every level they find ways to circumvent it. Otherwise they ignore it completely. Do you know that we have murders daily in our Lucknow? Nobody feels secure, There is the Mayfair cinema here. Some students asked the manager for free tickets. He gave some of them tickets and to the others he said, 'That is enough.' Because, you see, he had to consider his budget. Next day those fellows came back with a pistol and shot him dead. Nobody was arrested. Everyone knows those fellows, but whoever arrests them will die also.

'Gangsters have taken over the university. They have rich fathers in eastern UP, who are gang leaders in Gorakhpur and other places. They send their sons here to study. These gangsters occupy the university hostels, paying only sixty rupees per month.' He paused, held up his thick fingers, and seemed to count on them. 'I can give you so many murders they have committed.' He raised one finger, which seemed to float in the air like Macbeth's dagger. 'You are staying at the Taj. Near it there is one Ambedkar Nagar. An engineer was developing a project there. The students came to him for labour contracts. They will bring cheap manpower from the Gorakhpur side, you see? They expect contracts worth lakhs.

'That engineer refused. He was my friend. Poor fellow, they shot him dead while he was driving home after work.' He lowered his finger and paused. 'We all feel unsafe, we are all afraid. These gangs are well organized. They roam around freely, carrying AK-47s.'

A sound came from the door and Mrs Ali entered. She was a lady of awesome embonpoint, with bouffant hair. She was dressed in a saree and a blouse with puffed sleeves, and appeared somewhat distrait. She was quite willing to talk, but her mind seemed far away. As she answered questions, she swivelled her bracelet and rings, and tugged at the pallu of her saree. Sometimes she breathed deeply, which distracted me.

I asked her about her connection with the Congress. 'In the UP, the Congress was the only political party for which Muslims voted,' she explained, adding anticlimactically, 'Of course it was then the only political party. Pandit Jawaharlal Nehru's family came from UP and my family was on excellent terms with him. My grandfather was a judge, my father also, and my uncles were IAS officers. So the relationship went on. After Panditji we knew Indiraji and then Rajivji. When I first met Rajivji in 1986, he was very open and friendly. He said, 'We need new blood, young people like you.' So I joined the Congress.'

She continued, 'Politics is the only profession where you do not need any qualifications. All you need is the ability to attract votes. Each party wants the maximum number of votes. That is why, these days, all parties, except the Congress, take anybody who can collect votes; it doesn't matter how. That is how the standard of politicians is falling. Now you have many illiterate people who are ministers or MLAs. But the Congress took me because I had the qualifications. I had long family connections with the party. We were sure I would win in my constituency, Badayun Zilla.

'It is a Muslim village. I am a Muslim. Also my parents and grandparents were all born there and they had always done a lot of good work for the village. It is among the most backward villages in the state. It is constantly flooded in the monsoon, it has no railway connection, no schools, no industries.' I wanted to inquire about the good work her ancestors had done, but forebore.

'My election promise,' she said, 'was for development and prosperity. I promised to set up an industry to provide employment and also start a school for the children. I worked very hard and collected money to provide a road, a bridge, a college and electricity, and to build a mosque and a temple, though I am a Muslim.'

The destruction of the mosque at Ayodhya, and the government's failure to prevent it, had made Muslims all over India distrust the Congress party. This was particularly so in UP, the state that contains the disputed shrine. Mrs Ali, in spite of her personal efforts, her family connections, and her religious beliefs, had not been elected. She agreed that the Babri Masjid episode had had much to do with her defeat. But she also attacked 'casteism' in Indian politics. The word has often been used in India as a synonym for the mistreatment of the lower castes by the higher. To my surprise, she used it in the reverse sense.

'Now there are so many politicians from the scheduled castes and OBCs,' she said. 'It was all started when V.P. Singh was prime minister; he implemented the Mandal recommendations. Now we see the effect.' Judging from her expression, she did not like what she saw. 'Now politics is all on the basis of what community the leader belongs to. See the lawlessness here under Mayawati. See the lawlessness under Rabri Devi in Bihar. The leaders have started to come from low castes. Many high caste Hindus left the Congress and went to the BJP. The Congress had a vote bank of Muslims and Dalits. That also has been divided. But the Congress is still the only party that can rule. What the public wants is a party that will provide a stable government for five years without outside support. Only we can offer them that. But we do not have strong leaders. If we find a strong policy, we will come back.' When I asked what she meant by a strong policy, she replied, 'Any policy that will convince the voters.'

★

In the crowded and rather squalid central bazaar in Lucknow, which, according to Nasser, Rudyard Kipling frequented in his Indian youth, was a street of bookshops. They sold books in Hindi and Urdu and were little more than book-stuffed holes in the wall. Nasser led us to one that really was a hole in the wall: its total area couldn't have been more than a hundred square feet. It was bursting with books in Urdu, some forced into shelves, others stacked on the floor. All this paper and cardboard seemed to have become animate and developed an independent will. It bulged into every space, as though to drive the bookseller out into the street.

The bookseller, a frail man with long, disordered white hair, a beard, and a markedly cynical expression, sat cross-legged on a chair at the entrance. A younger man, also on a chair, was deep in conversation with him when we arrived. This person moved obligingly over and sat on a pile of books so that I could take his place. More chairs were squeezed in at the entrance, where a few steps led down to the street.

Wali Aasi, the proprietor, is a respected Urdu poet. He did not move from his position. Unembarrassed by the lack of space, he supervised the chair operation with calm courtesy. He scrutinized us, meanwhile, with opaque and extremely watchful eyes. Nasser introduced me. Wali touched his brow and breast in welcome. He spoke in Urdu, translated by Nasser. 'I was born in 1939,' he said, 'and until 1947, I had the memories all children have. It's better that I don't talk about anything after that.'

I stared out over the crowded bazaar. Next door to his shop was a food shop; steam and aromas of various sorts emanated from it. The pavement outside was smeared with trodden daals, rice and sauce-stained leafcups. Wali shouted across to the proprietor for tea. A small boy fetched it in glass tumblers, too hot to hold comfortably.

Everything was now as Wali wanted it; and he spoke. 'Have we really become free?' he asked. 'I ask other people this question, because I haven't found the answer myself. In Lucknow and UP, over the last fifty years, there has been a purposeful attempt to destroy Urdu.' He quoted a sonorous verse, which apparently supported his claim. 'You don't see Urdu culture in Lucknow now. Once you heard the gentle and sweet sound of Urdu spoken everywhere. Now you don't hear it anywhere. In my childhood, the shop signs in Lucknow were written in three languages—English, Hindi and Urdu. Now Urdu has disappeared. Many of the people who spoke it have left Lucknow.' He quoted more verse.

Then he watched us, smiling slightly. 'Who are the people who you say have destroyed Urdu?' I asked. 'The government,' he said, still with a slight smile. 'All those misguided ones who hate the language because they say it is Muslim. They removed it from the syllabuses of all recognized schools. They replaced it with Sanskrit. Urdu is a modern Indian language, and many people speak it. Sanskrit is a classical Indian language, which nobody speaks. There was no sense in this. But the result of Urdu not being taught in schools was that there was no work for those who learned it.

'For our religion it is necessary for the children to know Urdu. Many religious books are in Urdu. Our Muslim schools, the madrasas, teach it. I taught my children Urdu because it is their mother tongue. Many people send their children to recognized schools and teach them Urdu at home. That way, the children still retain roots in their culture. But travel around UP: from Jhansi to Kanpur you will not see Urdu on a signboard or hear it in people's mouths. In Jhansi you might find a couple of Urdu poets, perhaps a bookshop.' He quoted more poetry, and then a customer peered in from the street behind Nasser, asking for a book. Wali started to look for it. I lit a cigarette and stared out of the shop.

Lucknow, whatever heights of culture it reached, was never famous for its cleanliness. From Kipling's descriptions, the bazaar had been dirty in the nineteenth century, and it is very dirty now. Strolling cows leave their excrement in the street; the waste products of the foodshop lie around the pavement outside. Vendors sell their produce from handcarts, their wheels clogged by decaying fruit and vegetable matter. The house of a well-born Muslim is scrupulously clean, and high-caste Hindus are supposed to have several baths a day. But a clean Indian bazaar has never existed.

Sometimes, in these bazaars, the colours are vibrant: deep, rich, tonal colours which capture and hold the eye. They exist in the produce, the trees and sky, the clothes of chattering women. In northern India, these colours are weak. The leaves here were dusty, the sky whitish with clouds and heat. Many women wore black burkhas and the fruit and vegetables, in various pastel shades, were not so much coloured as slightly discoloured.

Wali and his friend wore polite, deprecatory smiles. Nasser said, 'These gentlemen feel you should smoke together. I think they mean you should offer them your cigarettes.' These were happily accepted, and immediately the conversation began to flow. I had drunk with Faiz Ahmed Faiz and Sardar Jafri and knew the habits of some Urdu poets. I wondered if I should now offer to buy some liquor; but Nasser told me later that Wali was an orthodox Muslim as well as a poet, and might have been gravely offended.

'Why are they killing Urdu?' asked Wali's friend, who had previously been silent. 'Because they consider it a foreign language from Persia, and a Muslim language. They kill our culture and our language, so that they need not kill us. See what happened at Ayodhya, which is in this state of ours.'

I had already noticed that Wali had an observant and cautious eye. He now bisected his friend's diatribe, and said, 'The problem between Hindus and Muslims, even when it occurred in the rest of India, was never in Lucknow. We were together against the British.' He had a long memory; he was referring to 1857. 'But now this disease is also in Lucknow, and it has afflicted us all since Ayodhya. Now there are young men in the city who will kill for a few rupees.' The relevance of this was not immediately obvious. He added, 'Some Hindu politicians are rich,' and then broke off, saying, 'I am sure it will be settled.' He quoted more Urdu verse.

'In Pakistan, Faiz saheb was arrested because he protested that they were killing Urdu. Here there is a democracy, and we can speak out. It is terrible in Pakistan, where even the mouths of the poets are sealed. I think things will change in their own time. Every twenty years there are changes in culture.' He began to speak of mushairas, gatherings where the leading Urdu poets recite their verses to one another and to large audiences. 'Sardar Jafri told me in Mumbai that the great mushairas are no more and Urdu is finished. But Sardar saheb is old now, and depressed. See, there are more mushairas in this land now than ever before. I have been to many, all over. And Urdu is not dying.' He gestured around the shop, through which smoke now billowed. 'More books are published in Urdu than ever before.'

I asked him why this was, if it was dying.

'Because we will not let it die,' he said passionately. Several quotations followed, both from him and from his friend. 'In the old mushairas,' he explained, 'poets dressed in sherwanis, and except when they applauded, they kept silent and still. There is a story that after one mushaira, a man said to his neighbour, 'I am glad that it is over. For six hours I have suffered in silence. Now please be so kind as to lift up my sherwani and remove the lizard that has been biting my buttocks all this while.' This demonstrated the triumph of Lucknavi culture. You will not find such perfect etiquette at a mushaira these days.

'These days, who cares? Some of the young fellows even dress in jeans. As I told you, every twenty years there are cultural swings. Now two Urdu poets, Gulzar and Javed, write film songs.' I thought he would express disapproval. 'I also write film songs,' he announced proudly. 'I got 11,000 rupees from a pop singer for a ghazal, and a Hindi film producer, only for a couplet, paid me 30,000 rupees.'

He lit another of my cigarettes, and remarked, 'Why should we despair? As new aspects of culture come, we must absorb them. I may like to read books, but I accept that not everybody does. If the shops sell Coca-Cola I may not want to drink it, but I will accept that others do.'

'In 1995, I went to America, by invitation,' he said. The scrofulous boy from the foodshop brought in more glasses of tea, as well as sweetmeats of lethal appearance. 'I had mushairas in fifteen cities in that place.' He meant personal readings, rather than the classical congregation of Urdu bards. 'In Washington, a huge number of people attended. Even in Chicago, five hundred came. There were smaller gatherings. In Cleveland University, the audience was only twenty-five. And in some other places I read in private homes. One thing difficult to accustom myself to was that when people applauded, instead of shouting from their hearts, "*Wah, wah,*" they clapped their hands like white men. But even that I could accept.'

'So you see,' he concluded, with an explosive and final expectoration of smoke, 'Urdu is not dying. It is coming back to life, and it has a safe home in America.'

Mr and Mrs Biswas

The Indian Airlines plane limped through the sky for hours to reach Patna, as though unanxious to arrive in a place of such dubious repute. At the squalid airport I was consoled to be met by Manish Kumar, the friend of a friend. He was a tall young man with a small, authoritative moustache, the local bureau chief of NDTV, which supplies news to television stations round the country.

Numerous trees, dripping with recent rain, followed us down potholed roads into Patna. The town seemed full of buildings abandoned midway through construction, cyclists, rickshaws and dilapidated cars. The hotel was near a railway station and a main road. I could see neither from my room, but it vibrated to the sound of trains and heavy traffic.

It overlooked a garbage dump where pigs rooted: not the farmyard kind but great grey omnivores with tushes, manes, and wicked little eyes. Manish told me they were ownerless and sometimes attacked people.

'You want to meet Laloo, no problem,' he said. 'Laloo loves the press, he gives us tea, and sometimes meals also. He eats a lot, sometimes mutton even, but he is not very fat like most other politicians. You could say he is healthy and happy. The public also, they love him, even now that he is charged with so many offences. They can never believe that he is guilty.' He had summoned a few other local journalists to brief me. The oldest man present spoke for the rest.

'Our Laloo may be as guilty as hell,' he remarked. 'But he's not the kind of man who can feel guilt. My paper has posted me all over the country in the last few years. He's the best chief minister I have met, at least with the press. If you attack him, he may not speak to you for some days, but soon he becomes okay. Many of the chief ministers I have known around India have had the journalists who criticized them killed. Give our Laloo *some* credit. At least he doesn't yet do that.'

I noticed that Manish had no drink. I offered him one. 'I was very addicted to drinking,' Manish said apologetically. 'When my father died last year I took a vow not to drink.' I suggested a Coca-Cola. Manish seemed really shocked. 'No. I told you. I was addicted to drinking it. I consumed eighteen to twenty bottles a day before I took my vow.'

The journalists left together. A team from the CBI was in Patna, and was at that moment searching Laloo's official residence for evidence of his illegal wealth. 'We have to go there,' Manish explained. 'It is not useful to you. But I have told a friend of mine to come here. You may place yourself in his hands with complete faith.'

Soon after this a very young man arrived. His name was Nayyar Azad Khan. He had a schoolboyish look, likeably rumpled. His father was a journalist, and Nayyar had worked as a television interviewer for a national network. A few minutes' talk convinced me that the boy might be an asset. He was intelligent and knowledgeable, but not loquacious.

'Manish is like my elder brother,' he said. 'Our fathers were friends. I am a Pathan. My ancestors, the Rohillas, settled in Bihar many years ago, so now we all speak the Bhojpuri dialect, and our ancestral village is in the south.'

We hired a car and drove around Patna. Unfinished structures filled it, symbols of different kinds of failure. Many roads were flooded. 'This is a more or less permanent condition,' Nayyar remarked. Parts of the city might once have been pretty, but had been invaded by slums.

They had infiltrated like moss into the crevices of the older parts of Patna. The wild pigs from outside the hotel had relatives everywhere. The newer parts of town, though as hideous as most other state capitals, had been visited by the twentieth century and contained office blocks and rows of shops. After an hour we returned to the hotel, and drank beer.

Nayyar said, 'Have you noticed that the women you saw didn't wear ornaments? Jewellery, I mean? Patna's full of criminals, of a new sort. They go around in cars or on motorbikes; their families are of low caste, but quite rich. They have risen in Laloo's wake. But the young ones rob people, even shops, in broad daylight, and sometimes they grab unescorted women and rape them. You'll see very few unaccompanied women out after dark. Otherwise they'd be asking to be raped. The cops don't try to stop the criminals, because they mostly come from important political families.'

I said I had seen the same in Lucknow. 'This is slightly worse,' Nayyar said. 'Women have a tough time here. Yesterday Manish did a piece for Star News on the Biswas affair. That's front page in all the nationals today.'

'There weren't any papers on the plane. What is it?' I asked.

He explained. An IAS officer, B.B. Biswas, had been posted in Patna for the last three years. Earlier he was married, divorced, and then he remarried. His second wife, Champa, was twenty-six, exactly half his age. While in Patna, she alleged that a young man named Mrityunjay Yadav, familiarly known as Babloo, had raped her. His mother Hemlata was a politician close to Laloo, and of the same Yadav, or cowherd, caste. Babloo had been to college in Delhi, and had published, at his own expense, a brief and servile biography of Laloo, written in a sort of English, and entitled *Rags to Regime.* It was on sale, but only, I gathered, in Patna.

'So they are great pals of Laloo's,' said Nayyar. 'But Mrityunjay is often in trouble with the ladies he rapes. Some complain. Not many because they're scared. But when they do, Laloo doesn't like it. This time he won't protect him. He's been getting enough bad publicity already.'

It was a curious story. Mrityunjay, clearly an energetic young man, hadn't raped Champa Biswas once. He had committed the act on an almost daily basis for nearly three years. When Champa's mother and female cousin came to visit her, they had been repeatedly raped, and he had called in his two brothers, as well as various friends and relatives, for assistance. The maidservant, who lived in the house, had also suffered. The word 'rape' seemed slightly inappropriate. All these libidinous activities had occurred under Mr Biswas's roof, while he was busy at more sedentary tasks.

When he found out about them, rather late in the day, he asked his superiors for a transfer to another state, took Champa and their two small sons, and fled to Delhi. The government hadn't granted him permission to leave his post, and so he was suspended without pay. He then accused Babloo Yadav of having raped his wife and named Babloo's mother as an accomplice.

The CID had made the couple come back to Patna to file the case. They were now staying in the Circuit House with their children, guarded by policemen. Journalists had flown in from as far away as Delhi for pictures and interviews. In the dialect of the Indian press, Babloo 'was absconding'. In other words, he had disappeared.

'If it went on so long,' I asked, 'how was it rape?'

'You could ask them,' Nayyar suggested. 'The Circuit House is down the road. I went with Manish yesterday. Biswas likes to talk. I'm sure he'd talk to you. And Champa is really beautiful.'

He said this in an awed voice. 'I mean, majorly beautiful. It seems impossible to me that she could have married someone like Biswas.'

★

The Circuit House, like many others, resembled a shabby barracks. It had broad verandahs, and in a verandah on the third floor, Mr Biswas was holding forth to the national press. When Nayyar introduced me, he crowed with pleasure and said he had heard of me and would talk to me.

He was physically wispy, lemur-like. His small simian face worked frenziedly. Large, violently agitated clumps of hair twitched in his nostrils and ears. He gabbled his words and was difficult to understand. But he also seemed proud of his new status as a man pursued by the press. He had perhaps never received so much attention in his entire life.

'We cannot stand here and talk,' he said. 'There are chairs in the room. I did not take anyone in there because my wife pleaded for privacy. But she is now in no position to dictate to me. So you may kindly enter.' He unlocked the door to a minuscule room, made to seem smaller by the presence in it of two noisy little boys and four beds. Champa Biswas sat on one, dressed in a white saree.

As Nayyar had said, she was majorly beautiful: she had delicate features, long black hair, pearl-pale skin and a voluptuous body. Sanskrit poets had described princesses like her. But they had married heroes. She hadn't. Such hatred flared in her brilliant eyes when she saw Biswas that I sincerely pitied him. She continued to sit on the bed, for there was nowhere else. But she turned her back on her visitors. It was shapely, and as eloquent as an exclamation mark.

Biswas addressed it, and though Nayyar said she knew no English, the rage emanated by her body was almost palpable. The curtains of the tiny room were drawn, and a power cut had killed the fan. The heaviness in the air was not caused by this but by her. The children went and perched on the bed, one on each side of their mother. She did not touch or even glance at them; they sat still, backs turned on us like hers, and suddenly silent, as she was.

Biswas said he had been in the IAS for some years; he was a Dalit, and implied that discrimination had crippled his career. He had been shunted from post to post. At times his salary had not been paid. He gibbered on, while Champa and the children sat on the bed like a row of silent accusations.

But he was in no hurry. 'When I came here in 1992, my post was not decided. So I received no salary. I was therefore economically deprived. I was forced to leave my family in the village.' When he got a post and a salary, he called them to Patna. 'I shall regret that day unto my death,' he said.

'I am not an ordinary man. I think deeply. I am engrossed not only in my official work but my hobbies. I practise homeopathic medicine, astrology too. I predicted that the BJP would win the last election, also that I would be murdered. Now this seems too much likely. Babloo's mother will spoil my career. My family life is already spoiled.' He seemed somehow pleased by his situation.

But he had also become hysterical. A fine spray of spittle accompanied what had rapidly turned into a diatribe. His small hands clenched and unclenched. 'On 24 November 1996, at 4.30 p.m., I came home and I found Babloo Yadav sitting on the bed with my wife. There was hardly one foot of space between them. Later I demanded, 'Why do you hobnob with him? He is not your relative. I forbid you to hobnob.' She said, 'What you are telling? You are too old-fashioned.'

'Later I found her in hobnobs with Babloo at the gate at 10.30 p.m. I would ask, 'What you are talking at this hour?' She would say, "I am talking about the weather only." Then she started to disappear from the house for long periods.'

What Mr Biswas was now saying added a new dimension to the whole story. 'I came to know she had hobnobbed a lot with this Babloo between September 1995 and July 1997. In July 1997, the children also became too upset. My diktat was "No more hobnobs with Babloo from now only." But by then I had found out about the younger generation.' This was how he referred to Babloo's associates. 'There are many. They are truly evil men.'

His story became more confused. He said that his maidservant, Shefali, who was fifty-five, was 'a bitch and a witch'. She had caused all this trouble. 'She fornicated freely with the younger generation. The younger generation also raped my mother-in-law, who is fifty-seven, but in a good shape. Then this evil Babloo abducted my niece from her village and brought her here also. They would take her and enjoy in some hotel or other secret place. Babloo alone enjoyed with my wife. The younger generation enjoyed with all the other women.'

But, as he said, what could he do? He pressed for a transfer to another state, but his superiors were very dilatory about it. 'The police, even this my IAS, they are slaves to the politicians. Hemlata Yadav is a politician of the same caste as Mr Laloo Prasad. I was also afraid that the younger generation would hire scoundrels to kill me. Or they will kidnap my children and take away this wife I have. She also, when the two children became upset on 27 July 1997, became repentant and told, "I will not see Babloo." On 29 July 1997 itself she once more went to see him. I could only think to flee from here. My family and I escaped to Delhi.'

He continued to insist that Babloo had raped Champa. 'The case is filed by her, not by me. If you fornicate freely it is not rape but she says that she was forced to let him enjoy because of the threats made by him and by his mother also.' He struck his brow theatrically. 'In each state the politicians manipulate civil servants. They get the police and civil service to do what they want, all over India.'

He clearly intended to say more, but his wife turned her head. When the ancient Greeks made the Furies female, they had sound reasons. Champa Biswas glanced at her husband with hatred, and then stared at me, to my dismay, in much the same way. Her complexion was unblemished, her eyes clear. She had not been crying. Speaking over her shoulder, she said to me in Hindi, 'I don't want to fight. Against whom shall I fight? What will I get by fighting?'

Her voice shook with outrage and grief. 'Can you understand what I am saying?' she asked. Nayyar, staring and slightly scared, started to translate. I asked her why she had returned to Patna. Biswas interrupted her. For a few moments they both spoke simultaneously; he won. 'The police asked me and said they would provide security,' he said, 'so we came.'

'They may have asked you. Did they ask your wife?'

This time Champa cut across Biswas's sputtered utterances without looking at him. 'They asked me to come,' she told me. 'They and this man pestered me till I agreed. I clearly said I would never live in Patna again. I am in danger here. Now I wish I had not come, but this man forced me.'

'Do you think Patna is a bad place? Is Bihar a bad place?' I spoke as if to a tetchy child, and she realized it and became even less friendly. 'Why should I think so?' she demanded. I replied, 'People say it isn't safe for women.' She grimaced. 'If you hear this from so many people, why ask me? I can't blame Patna or Bihar for all this mess.'

'Do you want to go on with this? Do you want all these people punished?'

'Of course I want them punished,' she said unemotionally. 'I shall never forget what happened here. They are all sinners.'

As we left, Biswas said, 'She did not intend to be rude, but I apologize. I did not properly explain who you are. We are all under stress, particularly me. The children were threatened by this evil Babloo that if they told me what their mother did with him, he would torture them, break their limbs, and kill them. They are still mentally afraid, but children recover fast.' The children, perched on the bed, started for no clear reason to cry. Biswas snorted irritably. His wife, still as stone, did not look at them, or reach out to them, though she had delicate hands.

★

Manish was in the hotel. Nayyar told him what we had been doing. Manish said, 'Babloo Yadav is still absconding. But his mother and brothers are at home. Do you want to meet them? We can go there now. I have already taped an interview with her, so she will permit us to enter. Otherwise her guards stop all visitors.'

I was very tired. I would have liked a long hot soak in a large bathtub, a drink close at hand. But I knew there was no tub in the bathroom, and had grave doubts about the availability of hot water in the hotel. Also, the Biswas matter bothered me. Champa Biswas had not been very friendly, but she had struck me as a troubled woman, who had been cursed by her own beauty and exploited by several people since she married.

Two hours later I was even less clear. Armed guards had admitted us to Hemlata Yadav's flat. In a small ante-room full of furniture, I was introduced to a brawny young man. He sprawled over a sofa, his shirt open to reveal a hirsute chest, which he frequently scratched. 'This is Babloo's brother,' Manish explained. Beyond the ante-room, in a kitchen, an ancient, wraith-like figure sat at a table. 'That is Hemlata's husband. Once he too was a politician. But she has more power than he ever had.' Then our hostess swept in, a worried man at her heels. 'Her lawyer,' Manish whispered.

She was in her fifties, a handsome Amazonian woman, who clearly disliked being contradicted. Not only was her voice loud and strident, but incessantly in use. She denied that Babloo was 'absconding'; he was simply not at home. Biswas was insane, she said, and all mentally unstable people should be locked up for life. 'He attacked my son's reputation, and mine, because he wants this government to collapse. He also wants to make himself famous by troubling big people like us. You know he was married before? He divorced his wife so he could marry a schoolchild, Champa.

'He accused me of taking her for morning walks.' I started to wonder if morning walks, in Bihar, were a euphemism for other activities. 'Now,' Mrs Yadav shouted, 'he says I took her for illicit purposes. My son is a good boy. He did well at Delhi University and he will become a politician or a businessman in Delhi, some good profession, *and* he has written a book. What book this Biswas can write?'

I had only heard of the Biswases, the Yadavs, and their complex connection, a few hours earlier, but new aspects arose with each person I spoke to. Each of them was trapped in his or her version of events. I thought Hemlata knew where Mrityunjay was, as did his brother, but they were buying time.

Twenty years ago, this situation would never have been allowed to surface. That it was now a matter of public interest was some proof that democracy existed even in Bihar. All kinds of issues were involved: politics, women's rights, child abuse, caste, corruption. Eventually, one way or another, the truth, whatever it was, would be suppressed, forgotten or distorted to fit whatever morality was current. But this was a classic case of what still happened to it in India.

The government servant Biswas would disappear into history and what had happened to Champa's body and mind become utterly irrelevant. But I was absolutely certain of one consequence. When I met Hemlata Yadav and her son, I saw what the new middle class of India was composed of and would become when it was respectable enough to admit it was rich. It was possible that Babloo's brother would wind up as a highly regarded member of an uncouth and corrupt social hierarchy. He might well play golf at the Delhi club where my cricketer friend Bishan Bedi had said plaintively of his fellow members, 'They aren't decent blokes, Dom.'

Laloo Prasad Yadav

'Now you shall meet the most controversial man in India,' P.L. Sinha said, like a television compere announcing I had won a prize. He was Laloo's private secretary. We were in his house, which throbbed with Hindi film music from a television set. Outside, rain tumbled out of a heavy sky. Sinha's servitors plied Nayyar (Azad Khan) and me with food in various forms, and with very strong, very sweet tea. Our host spoke of Laloo's virtues as a man and politician. He was careful to refer to him as 'Mr Laloo'. When I mentioned Rabri Devi, he said, 'The CM is a most virtuous, hospitable lady. She and Mr Laloo are worthy bedmates.' Laloo had named his spouse as his successor, but only when his position as chief minister had become untenable. Too many charges of corruption stood against him.

Presently the phone rang, and Mr Sinha, having had a conversation with it, looked relieved and said, 'With your kind permission, we may now leave.' As we drove through the rain, he tapped my knee and pointed to a very small child, naked, wailing under a tree by the roadside. Sinha stopped the car. The child was brought to him: a girl, who wore only a cord around her waist. Tears poured down her small face. She hiccuped and shuddered as though she would never stop.

The driver, carrying her, talked to some bystanders. He returned to report. Sinha issued orders, and she was put into another government car and driven off. Sinha said, 'I ordered her to be taken to my home. My wife will see to her. Later I will call the proper authorities. In Bihar,' he explained, 'girl children are not wanted. They are killed or buried alive as soon as they are born. This child has been allowed to live but I think now her mother has abandoned her. That is what the people were saying.' He shook his head. 'Even girl children must be cared for.'

The car sped on towards Laloo's mansion. He awaited us, seated in a cane chair on the verandah of an outhouse. He wore a white kurta and a lungi, and kept yawning loudly, rubbing his eyes. I sat down beside him. Nayyar sat beside me. He had come as an interpreter, and in a hushed, deferential voice, as though conveying bad news, told Laloo so. Laloo seemed annoyed. He frowned, then addressed me.

'We talk in English,' he said in the language. Jerking his head at Nayyar, he continued, 'He no is necessary.' Then he glared fiercely into my face, surprising me. I slowly realized that this aggression might be some rustic prelude to acceptance. Laloo started to answer my questions, though Nayyar sometimes had to translate before I fully understood them. Finally, Laloo ceased to wait for questions. He talked. From time to time he punched my shoulder.

Once I thought he was speaking Bhojpuri and turned to Nayyar for help. Nayyar told me, 'That's English.' Laloo didn't seem to mind. He spoke loudly, with a certain tolerance, as one does to a helpless foreigner. In spite of the tufts of hair that protruded from his ears and nostrils, his skin looked as delicate as a baby's. He was like a large baby, who would always be hard to handle. But he was giving a performance; and he knew I knew it. He studied me sideways, but never looked me in the eye.

I had expected little from this interview, and in terms of information got nothing. Laloo spoke of the inequities caused by the caste system. He said the central government had never promoted education as it had promised in 1947. He had done so in Bihar. He had founded schools for the children of cowherds, and made other novel experiments in education. I knew that all these institutions had failed and were defunct, but Laloo said, 'My enemies tell lie on me.'

We were brought cups of excellent lemon tea. Laloo slurped his down, and then began to chew paan of an aromatic variety. The rain had stopped but though a faint breeze fanned the verandah, it wasn't enough to dissipate the strong, sickly smell of the paan. Laloo turned his head away every so often to spit carefully into a bowl placed on the table beside him. Meanwhile his rhetoric went on. He had got into his stride. He gesticulated. He paused to finish his paan, called for water, rinsed his mouth, and spat copiously all over the floor. He said the enemies who wanted his death had lied, plotted and sent the CBI to harass him, but because the masses supported him, he had no fear. His enemies couldn't harm him, because he had saved the Muslims of Bihar from slaughter, rescued the Dalits from starvation.

Suddenly I saw Rabri Devi, familiar from photographs, coming across the lawn followed by several flunkies. She was a squat, bulky woman, simply dressed in a saree, with files under her arm. She waddled up to the verandah and went past us, inside. She didn't look at Laloo, who stared at her with a curiously sullen expression. He glanced at me to check whether I had noticed her, and seemed pleased that his interviewer wasn't interested in talking to his wife.

He then started to shout. I had been with him more than an hour, and realized that Laloo had to end his performance somewhere, and was perhaps in search of an exit line. Finally, I asked about his childhood. 'In the childhoods,' he cried, throwing up his hands, 'I had no clothesies! I had no foodsies! I had no bootsies even!' This struck even him as sufficient. He slumped back in his chair, with the look of one who has been emotionally drained. The interview was over. P.L. Sinha came to show us out.

III

History and Happenstance

Mani Shankar Mukherjee

I woke up to the sound of birds close at hand and traffic far off. A room bearer, splendidly clad in white, with a turban and cummerbund, smiled at me, and said, 'Good morning, saheb.' A silver tray stood on the bedside table, arrayed with the multiple accessories required for a simple cup of tea; it also held two slices of buttered toast, marmalade in a silver bowl, an orange and a banana. My friend Mani Shankar had booked me into the Bengal Club. 'Since it was founded by the Brits for the Brits,' Mani Shankar had said with heavy sarcasm when I telephoned from Mumbai, 'it should suit you admirably.'

Outside the window I could see a grey sky, trees and dignified elderly houses. Though I hadn't slept much, I wasn't tired. But I was very hungry. 'Breakfast?' I asked, and when the bearer nodded, went on in a gluttonous litany, 'Orange juice, fried eggs, bacon, toast, coffee?' The bearer said, 'Saheb, no bacon. Today Thursday, dry day.' The term had been used when prohibition was in force, for days on which liquor wasn't available. 'Thursday dry day for pig meat,' the bearer clarified. 'Bacon come tomorrow.'

I bathed; I had a baconless breakfast.

None of the power failures I recalled as common in the city had blemished the day so far. When I got Mani Shankar on the phone, I congratulated him on this. Mani Shankar Mukherjee, better known as Shankar, is small, bespectacled and slightly rotund: more like a business executive than a popular novelist. He manages to be both without apparent difficulty. He is not only a famous popular novelist, but also the public relations officer of the firm that supplies the state with electricity. This might be an odd combination of professions in another part of the world; but not in Kolkata. He was surprised at my congratulations. 'It was in the '70s that the power was off more often than it was on,' he recollected. 'My dear friend, you can't have been to my city for at least twenty years.' I realized that this was true.

I realized it even more when I went out. Kolkata was a different place now. Once, the red English buses, even the taxis, had been punctured and paintless (though they still moved very slowly). Beggars in hundreds had dragged their lost bodies down potholed pavements. Now the vehicles one saw on Chowringhee were intact and included smart foreign cars, and there seemed to be no beggars. Hoardings towered over the traffic. They advertised imported luxuries, very often mobile phones. A lot of noisy demolition work was going on, but the gridlocks around Chowringhee still existed, as reminders of the old disorderly city.

A Communist government had achieved all this. Its leader, Jyoti Basu, was voted to power in 1979, and had continued ever since. If Communism was a religion, Basu was a spoilt priest. Under him the Naxalites had finally been broken. Capitalists who had shut up shop and fled during the 1970s had been enticed back. Basu was now trying to attract the MNCs. I had interviewed him in the past: a small man with delicate aristocratic hands and features, who remembered that he had been educated on the banks of the Cam and preserved the fastidious air of a well-bred cat—not at all like Hercules, though Kolkata had once resembled the Augean stables.

Mani Shankar had a palatial office off Chowringhee. 'Shall we have lunch?' he enquired as soon as I had sat down. This usually meant, I knew, that my host had an hour to spare, and that while we talked, the office boy would visit a small restaurant nearby and return with an interesting and inventive mixture of Chinese and Bangla dishes. It was a wise way to have lunch. It avoided unnecessary movement and saved time. While we waited for the boy to come back, Mani Shankar took off his glasses, polished them, put them back on and beamed. 'So you've come to see how Kolkata's doing.' The beam dwindled and changed into a sardonic smile. 'Well, when the British left, Bengal was doing better than any other state in India. Now it's not even sixth in the country. Everything's changed for the worse. So the Bengalis who once loved change, have become afraid of it. We've had the same government here for twenty years, but that doesn't show stability, only terror of change.

'About 1947, when I was a boy, we had a neighbour who was a clerk in a British company. He was fond of me and talked to me about what happened in his office. One day he said, "I am very worried. Today one of the sahebs told me, 'You people wanted us to go, so we're going. But the day won't be far off when you'll plead with us to come back.'" Mani Shankar paused and stared at me. 'For years,' he said, 'I laughed about this, but today I don't. It was always a very strange relationship, theirs and ours, if you think about it.

'We thought they were the source of all our evils, and they thought God had given them the responsibility of looking after an inferior race. The truth lies somewhere in-between. The British were organized, with higher standards of education than we had. They left posterity a coherent account of their doings here. We've had half a century of independence, but our version has not been written at all. Nobody has explained to posterity why we wanted independence, why Gandhi should ever think our lives would be intolerable without it. Was it all empty words, prevarication, or the truth? Why was it, because of the errors of both sides, that we deprived the world of an

Indo-British culture? Was it the Mutiny of 1857, or the heat and dust of many years? Or was it due to the development of communications or of a new system of exploitation?'

The office boy returned with lunch. This came in several plastic containers and comprised Bengali fish fried in Bengali mustard oil, a foo yong and fried rice with vegetables in it. We both ate well, and afterwards, Mani Shankar, delicately wiping his fingers on a tissue, remarked, 'If only foreigners could digest what we eat. Street food is very good in India.' Then he picked up the thread of his talk without being prompted. 'After the atomic bomb I think intellectuals felt that future wars would be different: economic wars between one country and another for a bigger slice of the market. We made mistakes in India after 1947. Firstly, we didn't want so many Britishers at the head of companies here. We replaced them with Indians. That was a mistake. Secondly, we thought we could cut down imports through local manufacture. But though we assembled the stuff in India, we still had to import the components.

'It took us years to realize it wasn't enough to stop imports. We had also to export. Some countries survived by export; they became the Asian tigers. But we said we'll neither import nor export. We found out we were wrong. An item that cost a hundred rupees in Korea was twice the price here.' I listened with interest. Most Bengali intellectuals I knew were left-wing. Mani Shankar wasn't, but Mani Shankar had always been an original. 'We saw that apart from a few traditional industries, if the world opened up we'd be wiped out next day, because we were nothing. This country of ninety million people, apart from gems and jewellery and a bit of leatherwork, it had nothing. We saw that those so-called great industries eat up foreign exchange.'

He made an irritated sound. 'When I was young we had some ideas about pride. We thought it shameful to be forced to devalue our currency. In 1947 we were Rs 1.75 to the dollar. Today it's Rs 40 to the dollar, and we call it an adjustment. We Indians, have removed some words from the dictionary. Like we have no famines, only droughts. Our people die of malnutrition, not starvation. The only interesting thing about India is that it's such an open society. We can find out our mistakes because everyone discusses them all the time.'

He wasn't trying to be sarcastic. 'That's the greatest freedom we have received from Independence; not freedom from hunger or freedom from political oppression, but freedom to talk. When the British were here I watched people ruthlessly beaten up for shouting some nationalist catch phrase. Many bad Englishmen came here, afraid because they were few and we were many. But there were also intellectuals who saw good points in India and always spoke bluntly, never deviously. We've inherited a bit of it, at least here in Kolkata, where some voices have always spoken out, in defence of the Naxals or whatever, and opposed public opinion. We developed an intellectual upper class. It is called the bhadralok. It produced Tagore and made the city receptive to new movements. Even the Ananda Marg, who were called terrorists and murderers a few years ago, have found a home here. You should meet them. I'll fix it.'

Mani Shankar giggled. Then he glanced at his watch and said, 'I have a conference in a few minutes, but let's meet again soon. I haven't said very much about Kolkata. Do you know that about half a million people in the prime of life were recently retrenched in this city? No, that's yet another word that we Indians have removed from the dictionary. Now it's replaced by "voluntarily retired."' He gestured at the empty containers and glasses on the desk, the remnants of lunch. 'If you look at the statistics, a large number of Indian citizens can't afford to eat lunch, a very large number. They also don't have any drinking water.'

As we said our goodbyes, he remarked, 'These people are what you should discuss before you deal with any other aspect of India. Possibly, if you can, you should discuss it with *them*. But you can't. You have nothing in common with them, not even a language. It's a great pity.'

Ashok Mitra

Ashok Mitra is one of the best known economists in India, and very much a Bengali. He received me in his flat, to which he was confined with a fractured foot. The flat had paintings and books in it, apart from Ashok Mitra himself. Seated on cushions, his shrouded foot raised to rest on a stool, he was eating a breakfast of hot jalebis.

He had been Mrs Gandhi's economic adviser. I felt a long way away from Mahashweta Devi's red spiral staircase and tabby cat. She had represented one of the several real Indias; Mitra's was different. Two supplicants had come to see him, as they come to see any powerful Indian. Mitra dealt laconically, rapidly and uncooperatively with whatever requests they had to make. Then he had himself assisted to his feet, and hobbled ahead to an austere study. Arriving there, he seated himself at a desk and said, 'India was a mistake.'

He continued, speaking quickly, his face and hands part of the conversation. 'We have talked of the European heritage, European culture, but not of a European polity. Europe is composed of twenty or so nations, who are trying for European unity and a common polity. They are finding it very hard. Similarly we have talked of Indian culture and so on, but the integrated India our schoolbooks show in maps never existed, so no Indian polity exists.

'Through the imperial concept, the British imposed a unified administration on an area they called India. When they left, we thought we'd continue the colonial experiment, but we called it a democracy. For the first thirty years we managed, more or less, because of the charisma, the miasma, call it what you like, of the Nehru family. Once that disappeared, things changed completely. All that we have now is a desperate attempt to work out a compromise, which we could still describe as India. The last decade represents this compromise.' He flourished an accusatory finger. 'Globalization is the single complicating factor in this.'

He had watched reality through statistics, and the conclusions he had come to were the same ones Mahashweta Devi had reached through watching tribals. 'Liberalization,' he said, 'has not led to any improvement whatever in the overall economic condition of the people. But the top 10 per cent have never had it so good. And from looking at the advertisements on billboards and TV, from looking at all the stuff in shops, the other 90 per cent have started to ask, "If those rascals can have so much in life, why can't we?" Discontent breeds, and the scoundrels who become political leaders exploit it.

'The upper class, the elite, the movers and shakers, are perfectly happy with all this. In the last decade they have made more money than ever. They don't care what kind of politics exists so long as India is safe from globalization. It has become part of the political strategy to keep the masses illiterate. Some American woman wrote yet another biography of Mrs Gandhi. She quoted Mrs Gandhi as saying literacy was not as important as industrial growth. The government never set a target date to wipe out illiteracy. So the vote bank stays intact.'

The morning ritual commenced. Tea came, and biscuits; I had somehow not expected this in Mitra's household. He continued, 'Unfortunately, history dictates that the environment change. You can keep the Dalits away from schoolbooks for thirty years, but they imbibe attitudes from the environment:

they become street-smart. The representatives I see daily in Parliament will not continue as leaders if the people become aware of the depths of their corruption.

'You ask why the masses have never revolted. The Indian polity has an inbuilt mechanism to ensure that no organized people's movement can succeed. You have a central authority. The defence forces are centralized; money is centralized, so you can only have small localized rebellions. But nowadays you can gather resources from somewhere else, and this has in fact happened in places like Punjab, Kashmir and NEFA, the North-East Frontier Agency. I think, in perhaps another decade, there will be violent unrest in several different parts of the country. Disintegration will start then.'

'The economy has been in a state of near stagnation for the last half century,' Mitra said. 'Per capita income growth is 1.5 per cent per annum, but most of this, has drifted to the top 10 per cent. The masses have not got anything in a relative sense. When this is realized and we face the consequences of liberalization, there are bound to be deep disturbances in the country, even conditions of famine.

'The 10 per cent would still love to consume foreign luxury goods. But our exports are dropping, so that we can't earn enough to buy foreign goods. There is constant pressure to increase our exports. How does one do this? By the export of food grains and pulses. In 1947 and '48 the annual pulse production was about ten million tons, and fifty years later it's about the same. Why? Nobody's interested. The rich by and large aren't dependent on pulses, but the poor are. Pulses provide the protein intake for most poor families. So nobody bothers to raise pulse production. The poor can't pay good prices.'

He gave his bandaged foot, which rested on a stool, an irritated glare. 'Over the same period, food grain production, of rice, wheat and so on, leapt up by as much as 500 per cent. Yet the moment we need to step up exports, we export pulses to the Middle East. So the poor find there is not enough for them. And under such conditions there may be famine, there may be revolution. You ask who will lead it? A revolutionary movement creates its own leadership, I think.'

'You said when we started, that India was a mistake,' I observed. Before I could say more, Mitra was in full spate. 'What is India?' he demanded. 'People in Uttar Pradesh and Rajasthan actually believe that the god Ram was born in Ayodhya. So they live in prehistoric times. In Mumbai people are desperate to reach the twenty-second century. This is too great a heterogeneity to clamp together in a single polity. You can effect a compromise. You assuage the extremes of dissatisfaction that arise from time to time here and there. You pull your resources away from economic development and shower them on the states to restore law and order.

'The Punjab government owes 8,000 crores to the centre because it had to pay to fight terrorism. Punjab doesn't have to return the money. What about Bihar, Orissa? The centre can no longer hold except by paying blackmail to various states. Each time it happens, the chances of economic development dwindle.' He smiled as though the prospect amused him. 'Now we are in a state of partial anarchy. We can continue like this. Or it may happen that a strong man takes help from outside and tries to hold the country together. Or we may agree to some kind of loose confederation.' He shifted uncomfortably in his chair.

'If we continue as we are, the problem will only become more intractable with time. Hatred between groups will increase. No single formula can work for India. The alternative is simple. When the Chinese army in 1962 wanted to complete its invasion of India, Chairman Mao called it back. He is rumoured to have said to his Politburo, "India is already overripe. It's started to rot. Let it rot a little more, and it will fall without any help from us."'

K.P.S. Gill

Indira Gandhi took the blame for the desecration of the Golden Temple. She also paid the penalty. Now K.P.S. Gill, a tall Sikh policeman who had been praised for his disinfection of the Punjab, was suffering for an unconnected reason. Gill is widely known to be a hard drinker, and he is also known to like pretty women around him. At a celebration in Chandigarh, while he was still the police chief, he had offended a woman IAS officer, married to another IAS officer. What he had apparently done was cheerfully slap her bottom. A scandalized press reported that he had 'touched her intimately,' which sounded worse. The lady took Gill to court, and pursued her case over the years as fervently as he had chased terrorists.

He had recently been found guilty, and given a token sentence. 'He comes here often,' Arvind, a journalist friend, told me at the Delhi Press Club. 'But now he's like a broken man. This matter has been pending in the courts for years and it was treated as a joke. But as soon as he was found guilty people started to treat him cruelly. They no longer ask him to parties. Once Gill was at every party. Now you hardly see him at any. Indian society is like that. Perhaps he feels too embarrassed to attend.'

He meditated for a while and concluded, 'I think it is maybe too harsh a punishment. After all he did not actually do much to this lady. I think his misfortune was that he didn't pick someone else. This lady is a very strong feminist. And she has really damaged Gill's life. Look at this recent development.'

He was referring to an announcement in the papers that day. Because Gill had served a token prison sentence, he could not take up his new appointment (to NEFA to tackle the Bodo insurgents in the north-east). His chances of once more being hailed as a hero had ended; and it was an extremely anticlimactic conclusion. Arvind shook his head sadly. 'Poor Gill,' he sighed, 'poor fellow. Now the only official post he has is as the president of the Indian Hockey Federation.'

Next day I phoned K.P.S. Gill. The deep, sepulchral voice that answered wanted to know if I was Dom Moraes the poet. When this had been confirmed the voice said, 'I have read your poetry. You are at the Maurya? I like the food there; I will lunch with you. Tell them I will bring my full security.' Sarayu called up Protima Vasan, a friendly senior manager, to pass Gill's message on and to ask her what food he might like.

Mrs Vasan suggested the Bukhara, an Afghan restaurant. 'The hotel,' she said, 'would be pleased to pay for it. Mr Gill is a great celebrity. Besides,' she added kindly, 'unless you buy a couple of bottles of Scotch and take him to your room, it will be terribly expensive. You know what Scotch costs in the hotel. He drinks a lot of it.'

An hour later, a stranger phoned. I had met him briefly at the Press Club. 'I hear K.P.S. Gill is lunching with you,' he said, to my astonishment. 'Do you know he is called 'The Butcher of Punjab'? He is as violent as Bhindranwale. How can you break bread with such a person? Are you not aware of his reputation with the ladies? He may molest your collaborator. My friend was in NEFA while Gill was posted there, many years ago. He was saying that someone he knew saw Gill kick a prisoner to death with his bare boots.'

★

I was at the entrance when, precisely on time, a large armoured car drew up outside it, and a number of armed commandos leapt out. Gill's person emerged more slowly, preceded by his legs, very long, though not disproportionately so, for he towered over everyone else around him. But he was also lean of build. With his white beard and elegant turban he had attained the ascetic look of many elderly Sikhs.

The guards, carrying walkie-talkies as well as Sten guns, fanned out around us as we walked towards the Bukhara.

Gill had the long delicate kind of hands that some people call artistic. With them he rearranged the cutlery in front of him. He had not said a word, but the head waiter showed him a bottle of Scotch. Gill nodded. The head waiter poured a substantial amount into a tumbler half full of ice cubes, and withdrew. Gill's face remained still, carved of pale, slightly wrinkled stone. He lifted his drink to his lips.

Every so often Gill's drink was replenished without a gesture or word from either him or the waiters who performed the task. Relays of waiters fetched platters of naan, grilled and roasted meats, and daal. For all the pallor and fixity of his face, Gill seemed to have an excellent appetite. Between mouthfuls, he started to talk. 'I expect the terrorists to restart their activities soon,' Gill said. 'I'm often in Chandigarh, and I hear this from the people in the villages. I also had a phone call from Germany. There is a strong Sikh community there.

'The Punjab has been unfortunate in these repeated cycles of violence. One thought that after 1947 it would be quiet because there was so much bloodshed then. I thought we'd finished terrorism in 1993, but now I think it may come back. The Akalis in Punjab have spoken of violence, of trying to end violence. They've never used the word "terrorism". Unless you identify a disease correctly, how can you cure it? You may win the battle of the heart, but the battle for the mind has to be fought by politicians not policemen. Every political party in this country suffers from the same malady. All its members want to do is make money. They have no time for other matters. It will take generations for us to breed honest politicians.'

He had recently published a book in which he predicted that terrorism would soon return. 'What we most need is education. See, you have Sikhs who are educated, travel abroad, do well, but they come from the cities. They have at least had an opportunity for some kind of education. But you take the same kind of boy in rural Punjab. The green revolution took place there; the people should be prosperous. They aren't because so many remained uneducated, and didn't know what to do with money. That is the greatest inequality, education.'

While he spoke, he continued to move the cutlery around, as though shifting chessmen on a board. He explained what had happened in Punjab. 'But it has all boiled down to a matter of political necessities. The politicians make and break so many promises that the people are in perpetual confusion. The other day in a village I found an angry crowd of farmers. They said, "The government promised us free electricity. But there is no electricity supply at all." The next promise was free schools. Where are they?'

I liked and respected Gill. He had a fastidious intelligence, and was a civilized man, well read. Some of his actions had provided his critics with heavy ammunition, but I felt that this was his nature, arrogant and unwise in a way that Yeats would have approved of.

'Recently some Sikh boys from Ludhiana, fifteen-year-olds, went to Lahore. In the gurudwara, they met people who had fled across the Indian border. They indoctrinated the boys, who came back and attacked a Border Security Force post. They killed a sentry. The BSF didn't want to admit a mob of children had killed a BSF sentry in broad daylight. They swore he had been killed in a fall from a water tower.

Terrorism is coming back but it gets hidden. There have been all these explosions at public places in Delhi. Who is responsible for those?'

Over the past few months, random bomb blasts had taken place in the capital, shaken supermarkets, offices, banks, places likely to be crowded. Surprisingly few people had died. 'The Indian psyche is full of suppressed violence,' Gill remarked. 'Now in all this chaos and frustration, it's started to come out. Delhi and Mumbai have become violent cities. Some of this activity is terrorist, but it gets lost in the context. Guerrilla warfare is in the nature of the Sikhs; the religion tells them to fight for a cause. They harassed the Mughals in this way. The terrorists carried out a guerrilla war against us, and it became almost a civil war.'

He had not only been in active combat with terrorists, but was considered by the police of other countries an expert on the matter. 'You could say that terrorism is the symptom of a sickness. Violence is now very commonplace. What has become very important is the new mafia that has emerged in Indian cities. Every country in the world has its mafia, and there are several countries where the mafia is better organized and bigger than here. But India is the most political country in the world. Here people enter politics to become rich.

'So politicians want money and the mafia wants favours. They oblige each other. This is the most frightening thing in India at present. Evidence exists that central ministers inflamed the Delhi riots in 1984. The Shiv Sena caused the Mumbai riots in 1992. Criminals were actively involved in those events. Most politicians are outside the law.'

He used these two words, 'The Law', like Baloo in *The Jungle Book*, as though it was ancient, inexorable and always to be obeyed. 'The Indian State will never be able to fight terrorism or any other crisis successfully. No democracy can operate successfully without strong leaders. We don't have any. Of those

available I should say there is no better man for prime minister
than Inder Gujral, no better President than K.R. Narayanan,
who is a diplomat and a Dalit. But they would not be capable
of dealing with a crisis. It is peculiar how the government, the
intelligence departments, the analysts, nearly always come to
wrong conclusions over a bad situation. Our national policies
are almost always based on wrong conclusions.'

We had now been at table for nearly three hours. The actual
meal had been over for some time. I had lost count of how
many drinks had vanished into Gill as though by osmosis.
But his voice was as steady and unemotional as it had been
at the start; his large, expressionless eyes were clear. He had
been as unfailingly and elaborately courteous to Sarayu as
some nineteenth-century Texan sheriff with a code of conduct
towards ladies. I have observed some great drinkers around the
world, but Gill's capacity astonished me.

'The greatest service that could be done for the people is
to educate them. The total collapse of rural education is a
major tragedy. All that it does today is produce unemployable
youths. They go into these schools and no dimension is added
to them. They could be called the unemployable part of the
vast mass of unemployed adults. The number of unemployable
people grows daily. The most immediate need for them and the
country is quality education. How will they ever get it? Today
the most we are able to provide, and even then not to many, is
not real education, but simple literacy.'

One more Scotch was poured into his glass. We were the last
people in the restaurant, and the head waiter, with a nervous
glance at Gill, whispered to me, 'Sir, the bill has been taken care
of.' Gill drained his drink. We walked back through the lobby
to the main door, and the guards fell into place around their
master, whose voice and step, now that he was on his feet, had
become uncertain. 'T.S. Eliot wrote a very important sentence
about education,' he said, and then looked bewildered. 'I don't

seem to recall it exactly at this moment,' he said. 'But it goes something like, "This is not like that." Can you recollect a sentence of that nature, written by Eliot?' His brow wrinkled with an effort of memory. 'No, sir,' I replied. I felt I owed Gill the honorific.

Mr Brar

Mr Brar lived in a leafy, sunhazed lane in an old and exclusive Delhi colony. His large house encapsuled him, made him seem lost, like a peanut in an outsized shell: a tall, gaunt man with a white beard and a blue turban. We sat in his air-conditioned study, walled in by bookshelves. Beyond it the sun was dominant; outside the window trees stood, and their leaves hung limp and still. But the heat haze made them shimmer and seem to move, almost dance, though the day was windless. The way they seemed to behave was a contradiction of reality. Through the window I could see Sohan Singh asleep in the driver's seat of the car. Around it, where shadows fell from houses and trees, other drivers and people of unascertainable occupation were asleep. This country promoted tiredness, sleep, illusions; it had been called the continent of Circe.

A Persian carpet and an enormous, very tidy desk occupied one end of the room we sat in. From chairs around a low table at the other end, we looked through French windows into a flowerless garden, with a spattered granite birdbath at the centre. A Gurkha manservant assembled silver bowls of nuts, crisps and spiced lentils on the table. He also arranged coasters, napkins and china plates on smaller tables beside each chair. His master informed Sarayu that the tables were made of Burma teak, and watched to see that his guests used the coasters.

No traffic could be heard, for the main road was some way off, but disembodied shreds of sound floated across the garden. The neighbours had their television on. I suddenly heard the voice of Inder Gujral, disconcertingly fetched by electronics from the ramparts of the distant fort. Mr Brar was pouring drinks: Scotch and water for himself, vodka on the rocks for irredeemable me. Hearing this voice, he turned from the drinks table and stared into space. 'What rubbish these people talk,' he said eventually. He smiled, but his mouth was hard with more than ordinary disapproval.

He sat down. He was not an uninteresting man: his library contained some rare books on India, and others that were simply very old. Some were in Persian, which he knew. He had been in one of the early batches of IAS officers, and had served mostly in the south. Then he had been a consultant to some large private company. Now, in retirement, he was writing a book; he did not say what about.

While we sipped our drinks, the Gurkha bearer fetched enormous platters of scaldingly hot mutton and chicken kebabs. I took them to be lunch, and helped myself lavishly. Then Mr Brar asked us to table. Lunch was copious, and absolutely unavoidable. Over it our host came, at last, to the point. 'I have read one of your books,' he told me. 'Now I hear you're writing a book about India. Are you devoting some part of it to the Sikhs? Do you know anything about us? You have lived abroad a lot, so perhaps you don't. I hoped I could help.'

His face and fingers, long and mournful as though painted by El Greco, became suddenly animated. So did his slightly high-pitched voice. 'We are an entirely separate race,' he said, 'different from the Hindus, different from the Muslims. Apart from that, a separate identity has been forced upon us. We did not want it. At one time we considered ourselves to be Indians. Do you know how many of our gurus were martyred by the Muslims?' Mr Brar asked. 'Have you read how many of our people were martyred during Partition, fifty years ago?' His pallid cheeks had reddened above the white beard. 'In 1984 the Hindus martyred even more of us in Delhi. It was genocide. This is what my book is about. But it is a substantial work, and still unfinished. When it's finished, I'll send it to you. It tells you what a Sikh feels about India. We have been betrayed by India for fifty years. Early in 1947 we asked for assurances that a whole and autonomous Punjab would remain in India after Partition. They gave us promises, but never kept them. The Punjab was divided. In the western sector, the Sikhs were massacred.'

Patriotic music came in wisps from his neighbour's house. The Gurkha brought coffee on a brass tray from his homeland. Mr Brar said, 'Punjab became the granary of India. It was Sikh peasants who created the green revolution. But they took away the water from our rivers to supply to other states, including Haryana, which was carved out of our land. When unemployment came and the young fellows started to emigrate, the Hindus were no help. Then came the terrorists, and Bhindranwale set up headquarters in the Golden Temple. At that time I disagreed with the terrorists and I thought Bhindranwale committed sacrilege when he took arms into the Temple. Now I think perhaps he had no choice in the matter. At least he was a Sikh. He had some right. What right did Mrs Gandhi have? In September 1984 she ordered Operation Bluestar. Her troops entered the Temple and killed Bhindranwale and his lieutenants. That was real sacrilege.'

Soon after Operation Bluestar, Indira Gandhi's security advisers suggested that those Sikhs who were part of her personal bodyguard should be replaced. She apparently replied, 'Don't you know that India is a secular state?' The Sikhs remained, and on 31 October 1984, Beant Singh and Satwant Singh shot her dead at her garden gate. They then threw down their weapons and surrendered, saying to their captors, 'We have done what we had to. Now you do what you have to.' In the van that took them to prison, Beant Singh was killed 'trying to escape'.

That night huge crowds began to massacre Sikhs in Delhi. These were the worst communal killings since 1947. They went on through a bloodstained week. Once they had ended, the Sikh terrorists showed their teeth. Many politicians and army officers involved in Operation Bluestar were tracked down and murdered. Bombs exploded in various cities far from Punjab. When the men who had killed Mrs Gandhi were hanged, the situation became worse than it had ever been before, until an uncompromising police chief, K.P.S. Gill, quelled the militant movement in the early '90s. Nobody knew how long this sullen quiescence would continue.

'In 1984 I was not in Delhi,' Mr Brar said. 'But people I knew suffered; some were killed. Others had to face new attitudes. The writer Ajeet Cour was thrown out of her flat and nobody would rent her another, only because she was a Sikh. Eventually she found a kind Muslim landlord who accepted her. The Muslims sympathized with us; they felt that now we knew what persecution was like. Ayodhya had not yet happened, of course. When my wife and I came back to Delhi, our Hindu friends professed to be sympathetic. They came to our house, but didn't ask us to their houses. It would have damaged their reputations if they were seen to entertain Sikhs.

'The relationship between us and the Indians has changed. In Punjab particularly, but even in the rest of the country, we don't trust the Hindus any more. Why should we? They have betrayed us from 1947 onward. They consider this their country. In 1984 they massacred us in Delhi, in 1992 they massacred Muslims in Mumbai. Is it surprising that our activists went to Pakistan to be trained? Churchill described the Hindus as a beastly race with a beastly religion, and I thoroughly agree with him. See what the BJP is doing. Soon they will turn on other minority communities even smaller than the Sikhs. The

Christians will come next, perhaps even the Parsis. In the eyes of the Hindus, the minorities have ceased to be Indians.'

He smoothed his lean fingers over his turban as though to comfort it. 'Also,' he told me sadly, regretfully perhaps, 'other people don't trust us now. Before 1984 we were thought of as soldiers, protectors of the nation. There was also friendship. There were those jokes; you know, *baara bajh gaya*....'

Most other Indians had looked upon the Sikh as a large, protective presence. But it was also known that he often came of peasant stock, and his responses, according to folklore, were slow. It was affectionately said that when noon struck, *'baara bajh gaya'*, he normally developed a touch of the sun, and behaved in an irrational fashion. Many funny stories were told about male Sikhs. Western visitors to India, laughing at their own wit, said, 'We have sick jokes, you have Sikh jokes.'

When I mentioned this, Mr Brar misunderstood me. 'Oh no, they were not sick jokes,' he said. 'They were very amusing stories, and they were meant affectionately. They were like Jewish stories in New York, which showed that a community was accepted, even loved. We Sikhs laughed at them. But I do not often hear those stories now. Sometimes,' he confessed, 'I even miss them.'

Professor G.S. Dhillon

Professor G.S. Dhillon, when I met him, surprised me. Under his turban and his wispy white beard, his features were drawn; he was very emaciated, as though the anger in him had burned his flesh away. For the anger in him was visible. It showed in his eyes and in the spasmodic gestures he made. He looked almost unbelievably like the sort of political fanatic described in cheap spy fiction. But he was the genuine article. He carried some books that he had written. He pressed them upon me as though, tangible in his hands, they would convince him of their truth. I glanced at them. They were shoddily produced, but that might have been because, as a local editor had told me, many people had refused to print them.

The editor had described the professor as a very intelligent man who had no audience for his views. 'He hates K.P.S. Gill and wants to have a separate Sikh republic, Khalistan. He's very gifted, but I can't publish him. We'd wind up with a RAW investigation. Of course, he's a harmless fellow. He lectures on Sikh history.' This description made Dhillon sound like a closet terrorist, and a rather stupid one.

But when I met Dhillon, I immediately placed him as a professor of the kind who used once to be found at Oxford. Amused undergraduates would watch such a man as he peered into goldfish ponds and muttered to himself. In his desk drawers, when they were opened after his death, piles of uneaten, fossilized lunches were found. This kind of man nurtures an obsession all his life, and leaves behind a book that might be thought brilliant if anyone could understand it. Dhillon was wholly misplaced in Chandigarh. In another place and time, his obsession would have been considered splendid. Here and now, it was somewhat suspect.

What Mr Brar in Delhi had complained of was substantially the injustice done to the Sikhs; Professor Dhillon quoted documents. People, dates and place names were dropped into his narrative. All that he said about the injustices done seemed to be true. He had researched them very thoroughly.

He felt that first the British and then the Hindus had betrayed the Sikhs, and finally that the Hindus had persecuted them. 'Most Sikhs are peasants,' he said. 'They need water and power. Our Punjab rivers provide the cheapest power in the world to three states around us. Before Partition we had five rivers; now we have only three. And because of the Hindu government, 75 per cent of our river water flows into other states and is utilized there.' He spoke with force and disillusion.

'The Punjab farmer is prosperous, they say. His prosperity consists of debts—I mean he has a great number of them. The only prosperity is from the pounds and dollars that come from our people abroad. If you go into Doaba, you will find families living in huge houses, but no man is present. All the men are abroad. Their houses are founded and built on the dollar. A few years ago I went to England. When I visited Southall I got the impression that the majority of the British population was Sikh.' He smiled tentatively, as though uncertain of how his attempt at wit would be received. 'Of course that is not true, but there are many. They are there because their country is being looted and plundered.' His frail body shook with emotion.

Whatever his views he was still an academic; he quoted other people to prove a point. 'When Machiavelli told the Prince how to govern a territory which has been taken from its rightful owners, he gave him three maxims to follow. One, do not allow the people of the country to be in a majority there. Two, do not allow their own representatives any power to rule, and thirdly, ruin them economically. These three maxims the Indian government has religiously carried out. Nobody will ever know how much the wretched Sikhs have suffered. The Muslims were hostile to us; because they were afraid of us, they martyred some of our people.

'We have had an even worse relationship with the Hindus. We need a Sikh state but they will not give it to us because they are afraid of what we may do. See, the Sikhs had genuine grievances and they wanted redress. They tried orthodox methods, they talked, they drew up memoranda, they sent representatives to the government.' With his tremulous, claw-like hand and glittering eye, Professor Dhillon could have been the Ancient Mariner. But it was too easy a comparison. It would be difficult to shake him off, but one might not want to. His hand and eye carried conviction.

'Next they had recourse to law, they went to the courts. Then they tried out non-violent agitation. All these methods failed. The Indian government had a vested interest in seeing that the Sikh demands for a fair deal were turned into a law and order problem. It called a section of the community 'terrorists'. It was able to sell this idea of terrorism to the rest of the country because it completely controlled the media. Now the Sikhs have very little hope of redress. Vested interests won't allow them a representative government because that would expose all the misdeeds of the government. Monsters in human form like K.P.S. Gill have won for the moment.'

'You say 'for the moment'. Do you feel that the militants will come back?' I asked.

'Come back from where?' replied Professor Dhillon. 'Where have they gone? Those who have gone to foreign countries will surely come back. Many are dead or in prison. The rest are here, temporarily inactive. But justice has still not been given to the Sikhs.' He started to cough violently. He had been talking for more than two hours, and I realized he might be tired. Before we finished, I asked Dhillon what he thought of Bhindranwale, but he only replied that the government would not give him the relevant papers. What papers he required and for what purpose was left unclear, but that name seemed to remind him of Operation Bluestar and the assault on the Golden Temple.

'The Temple has been attacked only thrice in its entire history, twice by invaders, Afghans and Mughals, and then by the government of independent India.' He had become angry and excited, and for the first time spoke stridently.

'When the Sikh peasant, our backbone, is finally broken, we will be finished. You who can get your writings published, who live in posh hotels and go abroad, how can you ever understand what we suffer here? This tragedy is enacted before your eyes and you can't see it. People have died in Punjab. For what have they died? Those people in the Golden Temple, they had to face bullets! There were 37,000 Indian soldiers all around them. There was no escape. They knew they would die. Do you think it is easy to die?'

Then suddenly, he seemed embarrassed. He coughed violently, in shaking spasms, then collected his briefcase and stood up. 'I have to lecture to my students in half an hour,' he said, 'so I will take your leave.' I saw him off. We shook hands. He moved away, then turned back and said, 'I have only one request. You may discount what I say, you may agree with the Indians who call me a madman. But please, at least read what I have written. Try and understand my people better. Please, Mr Moraes, at least do not throw away my books. Please read them.'

IV

Whose Eyes Witness

The Victims of Bhagalpur

I had decided the previous night that I had wasted enough time waiting for Laloo, and that after the interview with him was over, Nayyar and I would head north. We had brought toothbrushes in the car. The driver, Minhaz, carried a small cloth bundle that contained his necessities, and had enough petrol for the trip. We drove out of town directly from Laloo's house. It was raining hard.

Minhaz, a gloomy man, said only that the Bhagalpur road was very bad and would be worse in this weather, and that we should be prepared for a rough ride. The road was certainly bad. Much of it was mildly flooded and severely potholed. For lengthy stretches, where the scarred, unequally tarred surface had worn away, it was only dirt and stones. But there was no traffic, and Minhaz drove at speed. We clattered over potholes and rocks. Nayyar slept.

I tried out my Hindi and asked, 'Why are you going so fast, Minhaz?'

'Saheb, we should reach Bhagalpur before dark. On the last stretch of road before the town, the bandits ride after nightfall.' I made no further queries.

Beyond Patna we passed small towns with bicycle shops, street markets and a Bihari version of transport cafes. We stopped at one in Monghyr, for burnt fowl and chapatis. Minhaz, when invited to eat with us, wouldn't, 'because,'

Nayyar said, 'he knows his place. It's difficult to be democratic in India. Tradition is against equality. The driver won't eat with the sahebs, even if they ask him nicely.'

After Monghyr we entered a new landscape. A range of low, ochre hills appeared on the horizon. The road was now on a shallow embankment, raised above the fields on either side. The fields were smudged with muddy water, through which one could see the stubble of the harvested crops. As we drove on, the water deepened. On either side it stretched away to the horizons; there, mud-coloured water and sky fused into one.

So we drove inside a brown cocoon made up of clouds and flood. Housetops and treetops seemed to float on the muddy water. Here and there small canoes moved on it, jerky as mosquitoes. Emaciated men fished from them. In the reeds under the embankment I saw bamboo fishtraps. By the roadside, occasional clumps of houses occurred. Their inhabitants were as emaciated as the men in the boats.

★

We rattled interminably onward over the unmade road. The air smelt of minerals and decay. Electricity poles rose from the sides of the embankment, and from far out in the flood. Strung together by limp wires, they were reminders of civilization in this wilderness of water. Nayyar said, 'They don't work. I don't know who put these up, Laloo or Jagannath Mishra, but he didn't put in any power supply, so they have never worked. This entire area has been without electricity for years. It's like the floods. They happen every year but there is no flood control system, and the same pattern repeats itself. The villagers go to nearby towns with their animals till the floods subside. Some live on the embankment. See the animals there.'

Under the embankment a few buffaloes stood miserably in the water. Egrets perched on their knobbly backs, pecking out ticks. Rows of other egrets were poised between the defunct electric wires, small and precise as notes of music.

When we reached the next group of huts, nightfall was near. I suggested we stop and talk to the inhabitants. Minhaz shrugged his shoulders, resigned. He uttered a few laconic sentences. 'He says it's okay. Now there's no chance to reach Bhagalpur before dark. If the bandits are around, it's our bad luck,' Nayyar told me.

The people in the huts were from the flood area. They were about to kindle their nightly fires; signals of their presence in the coming darkness. They had stick-like bodies. Some suffered from rheumatic and intestinal fevers. A young man said to Nayyar, 'To whom can we complain? It is like this every year.' A much older man wanted a cigarette. I lit it for him, and he sucked at it disconsolately. Tears filled his small bloodshot eyes. 'I don't enjoy life much these days,' he said.

Afterwards darkness absorbed us. Unknowable masses of black water and mud slurped and squelched on either side of the road, unlit except for our headlights. In the tiny roadside settlements there were fires, kerosene lamps, grotesque shadows. Bhagalpur when we entered it was also mostly dark, but the shops in the bazaar were still open, candlelit.

We found the hotel, where two people waited: the local correspondent of the *Times of India*, and a wiry, bearded college professor who was also an activist for human rights and a Muslim. They sat in my room, made to seem even smaller than it was by a large non-functional television set, placed at the foot of the bed. Mosquitoes the size of dragonflies whined their way through the tepid air. Neither the air-conditioner nor the fan would work, and the already dim lights went on and off, but Nayyar had procured some beer from the bazaar, which helped.

Farrukh Ali said, 'You have seen the floods, and the situation of the people? When Bihar was part of Bengal, Bhagalpur was known for its culture and music. More recently it became known for its atrocities and massacres. In 1979 bandits were unusually active in the countryside and the town was full of criminals. The police came under attack from the politicians. But both the politicians and the police were closely allied to the criminals.'

The *Times of India* man, Sahai, named some politicians, some senior police officials, and some wealthy local businessmen. 'Now many are dead; it was twenty years ago. But under their orders, the police seized a number of petty thieves and other minor offenders. They gouged out the eyes of some and blinded others with acid. This was to show that they meant business, and that crime in Bhagalpur was under control. Then they were horrified by what they had done. The blinds were evidence against them. They put them all in Bhagalpur jail. Gradually news spread that thirty-one blinds were in the jail. They were released and promised compensation. Not all of them received it.'

'There was an inquiry and the officers concerned were transferred. After you have had a night's rest,' Farrukh Ali said, 'you can see them. One or two are still alive. In 1989 there were also massacres of Muslims in some villages nearby. One was at Chanderi. The Hindu villagers slaughtered 159 Muslims and threw the bodies in a village pond. Some Muslims survived. They are still there. Very interesting. Tomorrow you can meet them also.'

★

Dawn next day brought out a brilliant sun. I hadn't slept much because of the heat and mosquitoes, and was not at my best when I met Nayyar downstairs. The news was bad. 'Your friend Laloo has declared a bandh all over Bihar today,' Nayyar said, 'as a protest against CBI harassment. All the shops are shut. We won't be able to buy petrol. We have enough for now, but not to get back to Patna. Gangs are watching to make sure that no vehicles move in the town, or buy petrol.'

Farrukh Ali arrived. We drove out of town. At this very early hour, not many people were about. A muddy field by the riverside contained buffaloes and thin villagers, also small red and yellow tents which produced a grotesquely festive effect. 'Things are started by Laloo's people,' Farrukh said, 'and never finished. This was supposed to be an airport. It is being used, as you see, to shelter flood refugees. None of the things Laloo started was ever finished.'

Outside Bhagalpur, Farrukh guided us. After some time, through paths between thorn trees, we came to a village of dingy mud houses. As we reached it, human life appeared for the first time in an hour. Scantily clad children scampered ahead of Minhaz's wheels, yelling till the adults came out. These were mostly women and old men. 'Most people,' Nayyar told me, 'have already gone to the fields.'

These were Hindus. They smiled, friendly, and called out. But Minhaz bumped through the village till he reached a chipped plaster arch. 'Beyond this,' said Farrukh, 'are the Muslims.' Small houses lay ahead. Children came out to see the visitors. The Hindu villagers stood some distance from the arch, as though it was an invisible border. They stared after the car. They had lost their smiles.

Minhaz stopped the car. Men and women now appeared from the houses, wary as a small band of deer in the open season. The men wore shirts and trousers and the women mostly cheap sarees. 'I know them,' Farrukh said; they touched their brows and breasts in welcome. I was led to a narrow balcony, surrounded by excited people.

One of the women eventually began to speak for all of them. She had a pleasant face, but a wrinkled skin put her, possibly, in her sixties. Her name was Yasmeen. The men looked sullen and suspicious. But when I smiled, she was not afraid, and talked vociferously for some time. Ten years ago, she said, the BJP had had rallies in the district. Until then the Hindus and Muslims in Chanderi village were friends. They ate in each other's homes. The children played together.

'Few cultural differences exist between poor Hindus and poor Muslims,' Farrukh explained. 'See, many women here wear sarees like Hindus.' Yasmeen continued to talk. For some days after the rallies, she said, the atmosphere changed. The Hindus became silent and uncharacteristically kept to themselves.

A young man now took over the story. 'They heard that Muslims had been killed in a nearby village,' Farrukh translated. 'Then, next day, the Hindus beat drums in Chanderi and the Muslims were attacked. They were outnumbered. The Hindus—they are of the Bhumiya caste—had choppers, swords and country rifles.' The young man pointed to a disused well nearby, under a gnarled tree. 'Some bodies were thrown in that well. Then the army came. The government had called it in.' He wore a luridly yellow shirt. His face was full of the horror and shock of recollection, and so were the other faces around him. They all started to narrate their personal memories of the massacre.

'It is very confused,' Farrukh shouted above the noise. 'They say the army temporarily stopped the killing. Then they put the Muslims in that ruined house there, near the well, and instructed the local police to protect them, while they went to some other village where there was more trouble.

'But as soon as the army left, the policemen handed the Muslims over to the Hindus, who began to kill them systematically. You remember, as we came into this place, we passed a pond? The bodies were thrown in that. When the army came back, all the Muslims, except these people here, were dead, mostly in the pond.'

Another woman spoke. 'They wanted to leave here, naturally. There were too many bad memories. Those who had money left at once. The government promised compensation but took many months to pay. Even then it was mismanaged. Some received money and left. These people received nothing, so they cannot leave. This woman, and a few others, sent many petitions to the government, who didn't reply.'

An older man made some remarks, shaking his head as he did so. 'He says, even if they had money, where would they go? A few of them can read, but they don't get newspapers. There's no television because there's no power. Sometimes they hear the radio. He doesn't know what happens elsewhere. He says, so far as they know, Muslims are killed all over India. They know a BJP government is in power so now they have even less protection from the Bhumiyas. He says that recently the Bhumiyas said they would soon finish off all the Muslims that remain. These people live in constant terror. It's really,' said Farrukh anticlimactically, 'too bad.'

Yasmeen now took up the tale once more. 'This woman asks, is this any way to bring up children? Her children have been robbed of their childhood. They cannot forget how the Bhumiyas, whom they thought were their friends, betrayed them and killed them. They all lost relatives in the massacre. They live with that memory. She says, they don't know at dawn whether they will be alive at nightfall. It has been like that for years. The men have lost all heart and the women have to be brave.'

Her lined face wore no expression whatever.

As we left, I said to Farrukh, 'The old lady's rather splendid. She's a bit like Mother Courage, isn't she?' He said, 'I am not acquainted with this Mrs Courage, but are you speaking of Yasmeen?' I nodded. Farrukh said in surprise, 'She's not old. She cannot be more than thirty-five. But normal village women in India age early, and she may have suffered more than most normal village women.'

★

As we entered Bhagalpur, we heard loudspeakers blaring. All the shops had their shutters down. Sahai, the *Times of India* man, awaited us outside the hotel. 'We shall have to go into the bazaar,' he warned. 'Put a press sticker on the car. Laloo's followers are very strict about the bandh, and they are there.' He squeezed into the back seat. 'Two persons were killed nearby an hour ago. They broke the bandh.'

We had no press sticker with us, which proved a pity. The bazaar was like a burst beehive, spilling over with frenzied figures. A cacophony of film music and shouts came from loudspeakers around the area, and no other car could be seen. We were suddenly surrounded by enraged men. Some wore the badge of the RJD, the Rashtriya Janata Dal, Laloo's new party. Others didn't bother with any badges. They carried heavy sticks. Incoherent voices shouted, and bestial faces glared at us, like painted masks in a folk play. Then the sticks began to crash down on the bonnet and sides of the car. The sound was like that inside a foundry. Sahai bravely rolled down his window and shouted, 'I am Sahai! You know me! We are press, brothers!' Somebody recognized him; all the hostile faces around changed, and smiled, and a noisy conversation started. During the course of it, somebody promised us enough petrol to take us back to Patna, as well as a safe passage. 'It is most curious,' Sahai said as we drove on, 'how quickly an Indian mob can change.' Rather breathlessly, I agreed. Minhaz mourned the dents in the chassis, and estimated the damage.

Beyond the bazaar the town was silent. Sahai enquired, 'Are we not taking him to see the blinds?'

'Pleace, saheb,' replied Farrukh. 'The blinds are difficult to find. I have put out word for them to find at least one. Now he should meet Mahima.'

We climbed out of the car and followed him towards a ridge strewn with ruined houses. 'This was a very old Muslim part of the town,' he said. 'It was destroyed in the 1989 riots and never rebuilt.' He pointed at the ruins. 'On that ridge lived the educated people. Some were university professors. They saw the mob come from two directions and surround the area. They came out and tried to talk to them. They were killed, and their houses burned. Then the mob killed all the poorer Muslims.' 'Now some have come back. Houses have been built for them.'

★

We walked on for a little while. The small houses, identical and, because of this, somehow pathetic, were spread out at intervals over the squelchy clay. At last we found the one we wanted, but nobody was in. The strident sounds of a Hindi film on television came from the house opposite. 'She may be there, watching the neighbour's TV,' said Sahai. Farrukh went over and came back with a very pretty girl in very drab clothes. She walked with a limp. Farrukh said triumphantly, 'Mahima!'

She took us on to the verandah of her house and asked if we would drink tea. Soon she came back with glasses of tea, and sat on the floor. I thought she was a social worker, and did not much want to hear about her daily tasks. I could not understand why I had been dragged here. 'Her children will be okay next door,' Farrukh said. 'They're watching television.' I hadn't thought she had children; she looked virginal, with a clear, olive skin and large long-lashed eyes in an oval face. 'Tell him your story,' Farrukh said to her. 'He is your friend, he will understand.'

Mahima started to speak, and I was suddenly hypnotized by her eyes and what she was saying. She had been born in Chanderi and grown up there. She felt no different from the Hindu children who grew up with her. Two Hindu sisters were her closest friends. When the massacre started she did not believe what was happening. Her Hindu neighbours burst into the house. She gestured toward her throat.'They cut my mother here. My father there.' She slashed her hand across her belly. 'I ran out of the house. I ran to my best friends, the sisters. They threw me out. I do not know where I ran then. But I found myself in the village pond. Blood and dead people were in the water. My right leg hurt very much.'

Someone had cut it off. Mahima told her story very quietly. Sitting on the floor, she rolled up her trousers and displayed a clumsy prosthetic device attached to the stump of her right leg. I was deeply moved. It was as though she had shown me her breasts. I said, 'I don't think you like talking about this. If you don't, stop.'

She looked grateful, and stopped. 'She has told the story too often,' Sahai said. 'I will tell you the rest of it. While all this took place, the army had left the village. When the soldiers came back, they found her alive in the pond full of dead people. They took her out and she was treated. The officer suggested that since all her people were dead, one of his men should marry her. They were all Muslims from Jammu. One of them agreed. The media said it showed the gallantry of the army.

'Her husband took her back to his village and she had two children. When the government at last paid compensation money to her, he took it, and threw her out with the children. She came back to Bhagalpur. She had nowhere else to go.'

Mahima said, 'But I will not go back to Chanderi. I will never go back there.'

'She cannot go anywhere,' Farrukh Ali said. 'She has no money. At present a case is pending against the accused in the Chanderi massacre. It has been pending for ten years. She is the only prosecution witness. The government has given her this house. The minister of community affairs has granted her five hundred rupees a month. That is very little on which to keep herself and two small children. Her neighbours try and help her, but they have no money either.

'The main point is that she has no proper protection. She is the key witness against those who started the massacre, and they are powerful, unscrupulous people. She lives in even more fear than the others you have met today.'

Mahima looked up with a shy smile. The prosthetic device on her leg was still uncovered, uglier than if she had been left legless. When I asked about her financial problems, she shook her head. 'I do a little sewing,' she said. 'I can read and write.' This was very rare in a village girl, especially a Muslim. 'I was good at school. I had a dream that some day I would teach. I wanted very much to do that.'

'Surely you still can,' I said gently, but she only shook her head.

'No, saheb. How is this possible now?' She spoke with absolute tranquillity and there was no despair in her face. 'I would have to pass exams, and I have the children to look after and no money. I do not know what to do.'

She was twenty-four, Farrukh told me.

★

'Now we will see the blinds,' Farrukh said. He directed the car through various alleys and bylanes till we found ourselves on a forlorn and slightly isolated road. It had fields on one side and small houses on the other. 'One of the blinds customarily wanders about here,' Farrukh said. 'I think his dwelling is hereabouts.' We went to one of the houses. In the verandah a large man slept on a charpai. Sahai aroused him, and he invited us to sit on it while he sent for 'Patelsa'.

It was drizzling; it was also very hot. The verandah was clean, but swarmed with mosquitoes. Its owner, dressed in a vest and lungi, eyed us curiously, but did not ask questions, or indeed say a word. Presently, a small boy came down the road, holding one end of a stick. The other end was clutched by a middle-aged man in dark glasses; He had a sway-backed walk and made bleating sounds. His white kurta-pajama was very dirty. 'That must be him,' said Sahai. 'Yes,' said Farrukh. 'It is he only. They call him Patelsa, but his real name is Umesh Mandal.'

He helped Mandal up onto the porch and put him on another charpai facing me. His head lolled from side to side, and a reek of cheap liquor came from his mouth. He answered questions in the same high-pitched bleat we had heard from the road, but could not control the volume of his voice. Sometimes it rose to a shriek, then died away and became inaudible.

'I was blinded in 1979. I was a farmer. I was at the railway station with two other people. A policeman arrested us and took us to the police station. How do I know on what charge? The police do what they please. In the police station they blinded me. Afterwards they didn't provide any treatment, no medicine. It hurt very much. They locked me in the prison. I was there for seven months after I was blinded. Even now they won't leave me alone.

'A case is being heard against me. It has been pending for the last twenty years. But it is in another district. I have no money to go there. Nobody is willing to take me up and down to court. I don't care if they arrest me and put me in prison. At least there I will get food every day and not starve as I do here.' Even in the open verandah, he smelt like a distillery. But, strangely, he didn't seem really drunk. He pounded his fist on his knee and shrieked, 'They compensated some of the others who were blinded, but not me. Not me!'

Then he removed his dark glasses. 'See what they did to me! I didn't do anything to them, but see how they hurt me! Why should anyone hurt another man as they hurt me?' The empty sockets set in his head still looked raw and contused. 'Take my hand! Feel my head. Here, where they hurt me!' His grip was powerful; he forced my hand against the back of his head. Through greasy, sweaty hair I felt grooves in his skull. 'They had to press my head down hard so that the edges of the table cut into it. Ah, I was strong in those days! It took six policemen to hold me down on the table when the inspector poured the acid in my eyes.'

Lachchi

In 1981 I was still in Bombay, still more or less broke. A quiet, rotund man with a moustache, Sudeep Banerjee, came to visit me. He was well known as a Hindi poet. Though Bengali by birth, he had spent most of his time in the central Indian state of Madhya Pradesh, part of the 'cow belt' where Hindi was spoken. He originally wanted to join the Indian administrative service as a police officer. 'But riding was part of our training, and I kept falling off my horse.' He had become less adventurous in his ambitions and was now the chief of the Government Press and Information Department in Bhopal, the state capital.

I liked him at once. He proposed that I should write a book about Madhya Pradesh, for which the state government would pay me a large fee. 'I think you might enjoy it. The state is the size of Europe without Russia. It is full of tribal people, wildlife, ruins, and in the Chambal, in the north, you will find many dacoits: bandits, you know.' He grinned. 'We will of course want you to write about economic development, but the other factors I mentioned do exist.'

About a week later, I flew into Bhopal. After two weeks research in Bhopal, I felt ready to travel. Sudeep and I drew up an itinerary. We visited Gwalior, a large city in the desert, dominated by a fort on a hill.

At Gwalior police station, Inspector Mishra said, 'A young dacoit surrendered himself today. He was with Malkhan Singh.

Would you like to speak to him?' When I said I would, the Inspector issued crisp orders. 'Don't be surprised,' he said, 'When you see him in police uniform. All the dacoits dress like that. They take the uniforms from the policemen they kill. I think they have a weird sense of humour. Meanwhile, take some tea.' This was brought, and presently the prisoner was brought as well, his approach heralded by the clink of chains in the verandah outside. He was a tall, sturdy, boy in khaki shirt and trousers, fettered at the ankles and wrists. He was obviously not accustomed to these appendages, the farther ends of which were held by bored constables.

'His name,' Inspector Mishra said, consulting a file, 'is Lakshman Singh Rathor. He's known as Lachhi. We are doubtful about his age, but he's about eighteen, perhaps a year or two more. He had admitted that he was with Malkhan Singh, and that he was implicated in some murder or other.' He signalled and the constables twitched the chains; Lachhi was made to squat on the floor beside my chair. He was certainly very young: he had a shy, handsome, rather simple face adorned with a small adolescent flux of moustache. The Inspector said, 'Malkhan Singh is one of the most terrible dacoits.' Children peered at Lachhi through the barred window. They whistled and waved. One threw a pebble at him.

He looked abashed, and kept his face lowered: the chains rattled on his wrists. They were obviously heavy, and must have chafed him. He squatted there in silence, and the Inspector inquired what I would like to ask. The children hooted derisively at the window, were driven off by a policeman, but returned immediately. 'Why doesn't he have some tea?' I said. 'And please won't you take the chains off so he can drink it? They must be very uncomfortable.' The Inspector laughed; he had a very kindly face. He ordered the chains to be removed. Lachhi raised his face and smiled shyly at us. At first he declined the tea; when pressed, he drank it thirstily, but was still nervous.

When I did question him, his answers were shy and incoherent. He obviously could not understand what all this was about. The attention he continued to attract from the children at the windows had started to surprise and disquiet him: in this ambience of uniforms, officers, inquisitors and spectators, he had become nervous, like a wild creature which, newly admitted to a zoo, realizes that these circumstances are beyond its previous experience. 'He seems to be under a misconception,' said Inspector Mishra. 'He thought that when he surrendered he would be safe. I am trying to explain to him that this is not so. Having surrendered, he will be charged, and he will stand trial.'

The surroundings were not suitable for any proper interview. I asked if I could take Lachhi back to the Circuit House, since he might explain himself more clearly there. Inspector Mishra said that if an armed escort came with us, I could. He added, 'I have not yet studied the case, but he seems to me an innocent boy. He needs some kind of help.' He was obviously the right kind of policeman. Lachhi was chained up once more. Then he, two armed policemen and I drove back to the Circuit House. The fetters were taken off. Lachhi, the General (P.S. Dhagat, officer of the Government Press and Information Department, who had been assigned to escort me) and I withdrew to a room. The policemen stood sentry at the door with their rifles. Lachhi refused a chair, he squatted on the floor.

The benevolent presence of the General made him unwind. It was explained to him that we had nothing to do with the police, but wanted to hear him out, and he spoke far more understandably than he had hitherto done. He had already made a statement to the police, but what he now told us was what I wanted to hear, not a statement but his own story. His father had been a poor cultivator in a small hamlet some distance from the town of Alampur. He had wanted to acquire some land, and managed to raise some of the money by himself.

However, he was Rs 500 short, and he borrowed this from a person called Panna Chamar. The terms of the loan had been shady: Panna Chamar seized all the land.

This made the family destitute, and things became worse when Lachhi's father, shattered by all this, died. About this time, Lachhi met some other youths who had thrown in their lot with the dacoits. Malkhan Singh had recruited them, and they felt they would get rich quick. Lachhi's mother was entirely dependent on him: he had no way to raise money. He also had reason to hate Panna Chamar. So he became a dacoit under Malkhan Singh. Some time later, three gang members had ambushed Panna Chamar and shot him dead. Lachhi said he had been present but only as the lookout. His functions as a dacoit had so far been purely menial: like the other recruits he had been a hewer of wood and a drawer of water.

After the murder of Panna Chamar, more was demanded of him. The dacoits pointed out that they had killed for him: now he must kill for them. Confronted by the reality of the situation, he shrank from it: he did not want to kill anyone. His mother had been appalled when he became a dacoit: she still pleaded with him, through messengers, to abandon this way of life, which would end in his imprisonment or death. But it was difficult, now, for him to do so. He had only been with the gang for three months, and his knowledge of its activities was limited. But he did possess some, and Malkhan Singh would probably have him killed if he tried to leave. So Lachhi went to the police and surrendered.

The General seemed much perturbed after he had heard all this. 'He appears to be a good boy,' he told me, 'but he may be in serious trouble. Malkhan Singh is a very active criminal. Lachhi may be charged not only with complicity in this Panna Chamar murder, but in any other crimes the gang has committed recently. I doubt if he realizes what may happen. They may sentence him to a long term in prison: and he is only a boy.' We tried to explain this to Lachhi, who bowed his head. Looking at the carpet, he murmured a few words. 'He says he knows he has acted foolishly,' the General interpreted. 'If he has done anything wrong, if he is punished, he says he has to accept it.'

It was now late, and the police escort seemed restive. Lachhi stood up and held out his hands to be chained. Then he impulsively bent and attempted to touch our feet. The policemen led him out to the vehicle, and they drove away. The General and I looked at each other. 'The situation,' he said reflectively, 'has now become very complicated,' and I knew exactly what he meant. Lachhi seemed innocent, even the police had thought so: and whether innocent or not, he was helpless, friendless and alone. All that he had told us, I felt, had been the truth. He had trusted us, and he seemed to hope that we would help him in a situation which he had not previously dreamt would be so difficult.

This had turned into a business completely different from an ordinary interview. Whether we wanted it or not, we had a certain responsibility towards the boy, even if the only reason was that he had nobody else. 'We will have to ask about this,' the General said, and next day we did. The consensus of opinion among the police officers we asked was that Lachhi would be acquitted when he was tried, he seemed not to have committed any serious offence, and he was young: but it might take months before he was tried. If we stood surety, he could be bailed out: in such a case bail was unlikely to be refused. But if we bailed him out, what, the officers asked, would we do with him?

He would simply be back where he started. Malkhan Singh would not be kindly disposed towards him, which meant he might be in some danger. Alternatively, after his experience of chains and cells, he might be in a mood to return to the dacoits. Either way, it would be a very open and difficult situation, and without any other options it would be pointless to bail him out at all. 'They are correct,' the General said. 'We must not only try to release him, but rehabilitate him.' We had to leave Gwalior, and there was no time to see Lachhi before we left, but the General plunged himself into introspection and trunk calls for the next two days, and emerged with what seemed to be an answer.

Some friends of his near a place called Saheli had offered us help. They had offered to provide Lachhi with five acres of land, materials for a hut, seeds, fertilizer, and the occasional loan of a bullock. He could make a fresh start on this land : it would be his own. 'His father was a cultivator,' said the General, 'so he must know how to cultivate. With his own land, the pressures will be removed. And Saheli is not far from Bhopal. Malkhan Singh will not come after him, there will be no undesirable influence on him, and I can keep an eye on him. We must hire a lawyer to arrange bail, and when he is bailed out, we take him to the land. Then the lawyer will try for an acquittal.'

Assuming that he was acquitted, Lachhi could then return to the land, bringing his mother with him. Perhaps, I thought, he could also be taught to drive, or be trained to some technical skill. If one young dacoit could be rehabilitated, so could others. It all seemed beautifully simple, at the time. Neither the General nor I foresaw the difficulties which we would soon have to face. When we were next in Gwalior, we visited the prison to inform Lachhi about this. But he had been taken to another prison, we were told. The police were rather vague about it: they thought it was Alampur prison. The General bought fruit, sweets and books, and we drove off into the hinterland.

After many miles and misadventures, we finally located Lachhi in the prison of a small town called Lahar. He seemed delighted to see us and hear what we had to say, and childishly pleased with his presents. It was only a fortnight since his surrender, but he had become sallow and thinner; he asked if he could have a bath, since he had not been allowed one since his arrest. We arranged this; I gave him some clothes. He authorized us to hire a lawyer for him; the General provided him with some inland letter forms, so that he could write to us. Surprisingly, he could read and write, and the General's books, he said, would help him tremendously; the days were very dull.

He seemed stricken when we had to leave. He said, 'I have not thanked you.' We shook hands with him and stepped back to allow the policemen to replace the chains on his wrists. We had ascertained his mother's address and sent her a message; the village was in the interior, but she had come to meet us on the road as we drove back to Gwalior. She must have been young, under forty perhaps, but looked older; her forehead was lined and her mouth sad. She understood that we were trying to help Lachhi, but she found it difficult to understand why. 'Nobody in our village,' she said, 'has helped us.' She had sold a milch buffalo, the last family possession, to pay for her son's defence.

We sat with her on the kerb of a well a little way off the road, and ate sweets. Her initial nervousness subsided, and she talked to us frankly. The Panna Chamar story came out once more. 'I was always afraid for Lachhi,' she said. 'He is a good boy, but he is simple. He believes people. Born here, where there are dacoits everywhere, he had no chance, there was nobody to help him, and he listened to the other boys. They told him what a fine life it was to be a dacoit, how Malkhan Singh would have Panna Chamar killed and how he himself would become rich. Lachhi had no thought of killing Panna Chamar till these boys talked to him. He has told me he did not kill the man. He is a very truthful boy.'

Her own life in the village seemed to be very hard. She worked in someone else's fields to maintain herself. 'Before I sold the buffalo, I made a little from the milk.' She was somewhat fatalistic, but a realist: 'Why should anybody help poor people? Nobody offers help for no return. Why should any government help us? We are no use to them.' She didn't know who the prime minister was, but rather touchingly said, 'If you want to find out who he is, Lachhi can probably tell you. I made sure he went to school, you see.' When told that the prime minister was a lady, she seemed amazed. 'If that is true, she would understand the way I feel. All women have suffered for their sons.'

We returned to Gwalior. Here we hired a lawyer to arrange bail for Lachhi, and to undertake his defence when the case came to court. Before we left the city, we had yet another talk with the police. I had come to respect most of the policemen I had met: in this area they had a hard task, yet they remained human. One policeman on this occasion, however, seemed rather sardonic. 'I don't think it will be as simple to bail your friend out as you seem to imagine,' he said. 'I have looked into the file on the case, and this innocent boy has a price on his head in two other states. Rajasthan and Uttar Pradesh both want him for offences under section 302.' He smiled at me. 'That means murder.'

★

Lachhi wrote to us from prison. He sounded fairly cheerful, and had been transferred from Lahar to Bhind, where he was to stand trial. We were fairly cheerful too, for we had talked to several lawyers since our last visit to Gwalior. 'He may be wanted in other states,' they said, 'but this is a matter of police procedure. He has admitted that he was with Malkhan Singh for some weeks. During this time, the gang must have committed murders in those states. It does not mean that the whole gang was present, only a few of its members. Unfortunately they are not in custody, but this boy is. So they have charged him with the crimes, but it is very unlikely that they have any proof.'

'That is,' they added, 'if the boy is as innocent as you think he is.' It is very difficult to maintain implicit faith in another person's innocence if the only basis you have for it is your own belief in him.

Next time we went to Bhind, we visited the prison, only to be told that Lachchi was now in hospital. We found him there, rumpled and reduced, crouching in chains on a charpoy. Two policemen squatted watchfully nearby, their rifles propped on the wall behind them. The charpoy was in an odorous corridor filled with other patients and their visitors, and the guarded, fettered boy had obviously become a kind of public spectacle for these people. He had typhoid. He looked listless and ill, but a lady doctor assured me that he had been a model patient and would soon recover. He smiled when he saw us, but very tiredly. He was still officially in judicial custody: no chargesheet had as yet been drawn up.

A journalist from Bhind, Baburam Jain, had undertaken to visit him weekly and supply him with whatever he needed. The lawyer who was helping us also paid him a visit. The SP, Mr Vijay Raman, and I had a beer together. I told him about Lachchi. Amongst other things, I said it seemed cruel and unreasonable to chain him up when he was ill: also to be guarded day and night by armed police would obviously affect him psychologically. Anyone not a criminal, when thus treated, might well turn into one: a very young person would suffer worse than someone of mature years. Mr Raman heard me out with a slight quizzical smile. Then he said, 'I told you that dealing with dacoits desensitizes a man.

'All my experience in Bhind teaches me that there is no profit in pity.' He picked up the telephone which stood on the table and cradled it in his lap. 'I also told you, I have had to harden myself. However, this once, I'm going to give my human feelings a chance'. He dialled the number of the police station and issued orders that Lachchi should not be chained while he was in hospital, and that though the guards should stay on duty, they should not carry rifles. This was not only a humane, but a courageous action. 'You do realize,' he said to me when he had finished the call, 'that if this protégé of yours takes it into his head to run away, his escape is entirely my responsibility.'

Next day, when we said goodbye to Lachhi, his chains had been removed and he looked considerably more cheerful. But later we received a puzzled letter from the lawyer. The bail application had been refused owing to police opposition: Lachchi faced serious charges, they had said, too serious for bail to be advisable. Then we received a second, even more puzzled letter. The chargesheet had now been drawn up, and the trial was to be in the next few weeks. There was no reference to any Panna Chamar in the chargesheet, he wrote: Lachhi had been accused, with another person, of the murder of one Wali Mohammed. 'Who,' asked the lawyer, 'is Wali Mohammed?' We didn't know: all we could do now was wait.

★

At Bhind, on the day of the trial, the General and I sat in a little courtroom amidst lawyers dressed for a funeral. The trip from Bhopal had been eventful: circumstances had delayed our departure, and we had only started after dusk. Kamal, the driver who was as committed as we were, kept the car on the road for twelve hours in torrential rain. We had reached Gwalior at dawn, breakfasted hastily, and leaving Kamal to recuperate, went on with another driver. Halfway to Bhind, on a rough patch of road, we had an accident which fractured both axles of the car. We had had to hitch a lift into Bhind but we were here, and we were in time. We had had a discomforting discussion with our lawyers.

Lachhi and the co-accused, Puran, they had told us, faced a very strong case for the murder of Wali Mohammed. The police said they had six eyewitnesses. There was no witness for the defence. Unless something really remarkable happened, the lawyers said, the two accused faced long prison sentences. Lachhi and the other boy, Puran, whom we had not previously seen, were brought from the lock-up in chains by grim policemen: they looked depressed and apprehensive, but Lachhi saw us, and smiled in surprise and pleasure, and we had a rapid word with him: everything, we said, would be all right, expressing an optimism which we did not feel. Lachhi smiled. 'Yes,' he said, 'you are both here.'

After such knowledge, what forgiveness? The two accused stood fettered in the dock: the lawyers whispered and rustled papers; the magistrate, also in black, appeared; the court orderly, in a thunderous voice, called the first witness. Karim Khan was a shrivelled old farmer, a relative of the dead Wali Mohammed. In Wali Mohammed's village, he said, there were two factions. Wali Mohammed, a muscular young man, had been the bullyboy for one faction. One morning Karim Khan's wife told him Wali Mohammed had been murdered a few minutes previously. He had gone to look at the body, which was incontrovertibly dead. He had not witnessed the murder. Of the two accused, he knew Puran by sight, not Lachhi.

When Karim Khan stepped down, the General and I suddenly felt some hope. If all the witnesses were like this, the whole situation would be different. And, miraculously almost, the witnesses who followed Karim Khan were, if possible, less helpful to the prosecution than he had been. They denied that they had told the police that they had seen the murder. They denied, in fact, that they had ever been anywhere near the scene of the crime. They could not understand why the police had called them. Some of them said they knew Puran by sight, none of them knew Lachhi. The only evidence that stood was that Wali Mohammed was actually dead, murdered by two unknown men, one armed with an axe, one with a sickle.

By the end of the day, we had to return to Bhopal. The General managed to see Lachhi and to cheer him up a little more. It now seemed highly likely that he would be acquitted, and two days later, after some very inconclusive forensic evidence had been produced, we heard that he had been. He returned to his mother in the village, and some days later we had him brought to Bhopal. It was unfortunate that the only way we could contact him was through the local police. When a constable turned up at the village and ordered him to come to Gwalior, Lachhi had understandably thought he was about to be arrested once more but everything had been clarified, and at Saheli his new land awaited him.

Amongst Naxalites

The Air India flight to Kolkata was delayed for nearly two hours, and the reason for this was a group of nuns. They were burdened by bulky aid packages of medical supplies from America, which they were checking on to the Kolkata plane. The discomfort of the airport, and the damp heat, were trying enough, and many of the other passengers were Indian businessmen, not usually patient in the face of delays, whether or not caused by nuns. But there were no complaints. The nuns wore cheap white cotton sarees, thinly bordered in blue; a costume known all over India as that of Mother Teresa's Little Sisters of Charity. The aura of the Nobel Peace Prize, and godliness, had rubbed off on them. Nobody questioned them; people even tried to help them.

But the nuns declined help. They were frail, bespectacled, formidably impassive young women from Kerala, and once they had checked the last package in, they silently boarded the plane with the other passengers, and began to fill in forms for the Kolkata customs. They ate the inflight dinner without undue repugnance, then started to read their missals. I watched them as their lips moved in prayer; I remembered other days.

Before dawn in the 1970s, the pavements around Chowringhee, in the centre of Kolkata, resembled a mortuary. Shrouded in white, many bodies lay outside the locked doors of shops, or even at the palatial entrance to the Grand Hotel.

Some tossed in their sleep and cried out: a name, a question, perhaps a plea. Others did not move at all; some were dead.

White-clad like the pavement sleepers, wraith-like, Mother Teresa's nuns moved amidst the sleepers, shining their electric torches. They made note of where the corpses lay, so that the police could later remove them. When they found someone not yet dead, they lifted the body up, like a light, nearly empty chalice, and took it to Nirmal Hriday, the house of help. There the dying man or woman was cleansed, fed, enabled to die with a little dignity.

At that time of day, with the city not quite awake, other figures moved in the alleys and bylanes around Chowringhee. These were Naxal executioners, usually alone but sometimes in twos or threes. They looked for solitary policemen, tired after hours on the beat. The unlucky ones would be shot or stabbed, sometimes beheaded. Afterwards, if he had time, the killer would use the blood to paint slogans on the nearest wall, before he disappeared into the dark.

It was only natural that the paths of the nuns and the Naxalites should sometimes cross. If they met, they were unlikely to speak or acknowledge each other. Mother Teresa once told me that the terrorists had sometimes approached the nuns and asked to be blessed. I inquired if the sisters had ever obliged, but got no reply.

I met a young but seasoned Naxal killer in his hideout, a friend's flat. The boy had trembled throughout our brief talk, and chain-smoked as he listened for the police. 'After I killed my first policeman,' he said to me, 'I felt very bad. For many days I could not eat or sleep. But Chairman Mao's Red Book told me that this was only the residue of my bourgeois morality. So I was comforted.' He had killed seven policemen since.

I watched as the young nuns read their missals. To each his own. In those days Naxalites and nuns, on their very dissimilar missions, had been moved by similar principles. Justice and pity, differently interpreted, had motivated both.

This was an extremely arguable proposition. But it was now past midnight. The plane was on its glide path, downward through darkness to the scattered lights of Kolkata, and I had no time left for further metaphysical arguments with myself.

★

Next afternoon an unknown young man phoned me with an educated voice. He asked to meet me. 'You will not know me,' he said. 'But you know my father. He said to tell you that I am Monodeep's son.' I remembered Monodeep.

At the end of the 1960s, BBC TV sent a team to Kolkata to do a feature on the Naxalites. I came as the scriptwriter. In Kolkata I went to Presidency College, known to be full of Naxalites, to try and make contact with the terrorists. It had proved to be incredibly simple.

I entered the college, the walls of which were scrawled over with political graffiti, and found a pretty girl walking down a path. I smiled at her, and asked where I could find a Naxalite. She pointed to some shrubbery and replied, 'Their leader's hiding from the police behind those bushes.'

Behind the bushes a beautiful boy, a shawl draped round his shoulders, lay in the grass reading. I introduced myself and explained my mission. The young man sat up and said, 'I am Monodeep. I am willing to help you.' He then rose, complaining that his piles hurt. I thought this a very prosaic complaint in a young revolutionary who looked like Byron.

Monodeep said, 'I got them because I had to sit for hours on the wet rocks outside villages, waiting for my peasant comrades to give the signal to strike. Then we entered and slaughtered the capitalist landlord and his entire family. We used their bloody limbs as brushes to paint the walls with quotations from the

Red Book.' He seemed too mild for any of this. He agreed to visit my hotel, to meet the producer.

All the way there, he lay on the floor of the taxi, wrapped in his shawl, because the police were hunting him. The driver seemed remarkably unexcited. Monodeep climbed out at the rear of the hotel, saying he would come up to my room through the kitchens. 'Cooks are politically very enlightened,' he explained.

The producer and I were talking to him upstairs, when there was a knock, and Ranjit Gupta came in. He was the chief of police and the Naxalites had put a price of 10,000 rupees on his head. He was also a writer; we were friends.

Monodeep leapt to his feet. Gupta waved a hand at him. 'Sit down, son. I had a drink with your father yesterday. He wants you to come home and be a good boy, and everything will be forgiven. It's a good offer. If you don't take it, remember I can take you whenever I like. Today I'm wearing my postman's hat, but next time we meet I shall take you, and you will not like what my constables will do to you then.'

Gupta left. Monodeep, very shaken, followed soon after. I never met him again. A year later, back in Kolkata to write more about the Naxalites, I lunched with Gupta in the Bengal Club: brown Windsor soup, steak-and-kidney pie. I asked after Monodeep. Gupta, a civilized and pleasant man, could produce a cold, saurian smile intended to terrify. He had done so that time with Monodeep. He did so now.

'I took him, in the end. He's inside. He's only a boy, but he did some harm. He killed some landlords and maybe one or two of my people. So the prison guards will really have it in for him. I wouldn't like to be in his sandals now.'

Twenty-five years later, I said to Monodeep's son, over the phone, 'Come to tea this afternoon, at say 4 o'clock?'

'Thank you, sir. I know the Bengal Club. I've been there once or twice. My father's a member.'

★

The young man turned out not to have inherited his father's flamboyance nor his taste for ethnic clothes. He also appeared to know the strange, Victorian regulations about attire that prevailed in the Bengal Club, and not to have any inclination to flout them. He arrived in trousers—jeans were forbidden—a conservative shirt and tie, and shoes as opposed to slippers or sandals. He was pale and very young, only eighteen, but had a sense of humour.

We sat in my room. The room boy served tea, plumcake and cucumber sandwiches. 'Some years ago,' Samir said, 'they served crumpets. But I think only one very old cook from the British days knew how to make them. He died.'

He was in his first year at Presidency College. 'It was once the home of revolutionaries, as you probably know. Henry Derozio was there, the poet, and my dad. Now of course there aren't any. All of us are very serious about our careers. I'm going to America when I've finished, to study computers. There's a lot of money in that. Have you ever been to Silicon Valley, sir? That's where I hope to end up.'

He seemed certain of himself, but not sufficiently so to say why he had wanted to meet me. We had nearly finished tea before he came to the point. 'I don't know why, but since we were children all my friends and I have hero-worshipped the Naxals. Perhaps it's because we aren't devoted to any cause, and they gave up their lives for one. You know there's a railway station where fifty policemen under Ranjit Gupta once surrounded three Naxals. The Naxals fought them off for hours till they were all killed. Older boys told us about it. They said you could still see bloodstains on the walls and platforms. We kids used to go there, almost like pilgrims. But we never found any bloodstains. We still went there, just to imagine what it must have been like.

'I never thought much of my father when I was a kid. He's been a bit of a loner in the family. He's rich, but not because he's good at business. The family has an established business that makes plenty of money. He's a bit of a passenger in the firm. He goes to the office, but I don't think my uncles consult him in important decisions. At home he reads in his study, he hasn't any friends or anything. He's never been what you might call close to us kids.

'But last year when I entered Presidency my father gave me an old scrapbook. It was full of newspaper clippings about him when he was young. That's when I found out that he had been a Naxal. I learnt that Ranjit Gupta had arrested him. He was two years in prison. He won't talk about it but he once told me they tortured him there.

'Sir, after I knew all that I got to admire my father like anything. I used to admire my uncles but now I think they are nothing in front of him. But he won't talk about that time. Sir, some articles in the scrapbook are by you. You describe how you found him hiding from the police in the college. He was told you were here. So he told me to try and see you. He said you knew what he was like when he was young.'

I tried to tell him. I omitted certain details. Ranjit Gupta had thought of Monodeep as a dilettante, a rich and silly boy, not dedicated like some of the others who had come from poor families. Ranjit had thought of his arrest and imprisonment, even his torture, as the kind of punishment a headmaster like Dr Arnold might have handed out to a pupil when gentler methods failed.

Monodeep had been a romantic idealist, and perhaps only because he had been silly, he had also been brave. In sending his son to me, he had been brave. He had thrown himself upon my goodwill. I also thought he was brave to continue living as he did. He deserved any kindness I could show him. I was very careful about what I said to his son.

When Samar left, he said, 'Thank you, sir. Now I feel at last I know my father.' I felt that I might have done a good deed, but wasn't quite sure that I had.

Mother Teresa

Mother Teresa is a Catholic nun who was born in Albania but has lived in Calcutta for much of her adult life. She has devoted her time to working for the poor: her nuns and she, for many years, scooped the grasshopper skeletons of the dying off the streets and took them to a place where they could complete the short, dreadful cycle of their lives on clean beds, with food available, and kind people around them. She and her nuns also helped lepers and abandoned children and fed the needy insofar as they could. Mother Teresa was then discovered by the mass media: television films were made about her for the West. Malcolm Muggeridge wrote a book about her.

Her integrity, through all this, remained inviolate. She received donations, awards and funds from ordinary people and world bodies, and she funelled it back into her charitable works. One of these is a house called Nirmal Hriday, which means 'pure heart,' where the dying are brought off the streets. When I visited the place, with Leela and a svelte young socialite, Mrs Rita Dev Verma, who is a disciple of Mother Teresa's, there were seventy-four men and eighty-one women there. They lay huddled together, on austere but clean bedding, silent, perhaps too tired to speak, exuding the sweetish, stale smell of approaching death. 'I come here every week,' Mrs Verma said.

The dying entered the place every day. Some had become a little insane. A woman of about forty, shrivelled under a sheet, begged to be allowed to return to her home, though she had none. Some of the dying folded their hands to us in namastes but did not speak. There was an exhausted young mother with a dying baby in her arms. The exactitude of death prevailed over all those who lay waiting for it on the stone floors. Outside, the wreck of Calcutta, obscured by its slime of people, dragged its huge body onward to its own final demise. What the residents of Bombay fear their city will become, Calcutta already is— one of the worst places in the world.

Mother Teresa herself appears to have been slow to see that there were too many people in the city. If she saw it, she was slow to analyse the cause. She was opposed to the introduction of contraception to the people, despite the dying children in the roadways. Eventually, she decided to make her health workers introduce the rhythm method to poor mothers: they were issued with thermometers and by taking their own temperatures were supposed to plot monthly charts of safe and unsafe periods for intercourse. Two of these workers, Mrs Lovejoy and Mrs Domingo, took us around various slum areas, to demonstrate how their programme operated.

The houses to which they took us mostly consisted of one or two small rooms, the water supply coming from a public tap at which the wives started to queue in the frightful hour before dawn. The average income of the couples who lived in these tenements was between sixty and seventy rupees a month. That is about ten dollars a month, or four pounds. The average number of children they had was between four and five. The mothers talked to us, their doe eyes wide, about the impossibility of feeding or clothing the children, let alone educating them. They could not afford to offer us anything to eat or drink. They tried to offer us air, gently fanning the flies off our sweaty faces with their little calloused hands.

These women kept their thermometers and their charts; they clearly hoped not to have any more children. How successful the rhythm method had proved was difficult to ascertain. The women do not use it simply because they are Catholics—some are Hindus and Muslims who heard about it while taking their children to Mother Teresa's clinic. The workers tell them about other contraceptive methods but don't supply any devices apart from thermometers. Mrs Lovejoy said in a disappointed way that some of the acceptors abandoned the thermometers in favour of pills or the loop, though she did not explain why. The women themselves smiled a little blankly when asked.

But they looked, with their wide, harmed, harmless eyes at their children. In the small, dark, surprisingly neat rooms beyond the shallow sills of the doorways, the children played. Sculptured into the skin, their ribs swelled outward at every breath. The last children in nearly every family we visited had the swollen and weak ankles symptomatic of rickets, and some had the mild white stare of the mentally defective. Mrs Lovejoy herself had five children; she was a member of the community in which she worked, and her husband brought home eighty rupees a month, about eleven dollars. The Lovejoys, husband, wife and five children, lived in a place called Crematorium Street.

I went to see Mother Teresa in her clinic—a withered, wiry little woman, with vividly blue eyes under her wimple and a voice that manages curiously to mix Albanian gutterals with a very Indian lilt. This voice is very low and very intense, and when she spoke to us we heard it against the slow float of voices from a choir in the chapel above. In the courtyard outside an Alsatian basked on a leash in the sun, and the street beyond was filthy and crowded and fierce. 'Why are people so worried about world population?' Mother Teresa asked. 'There is plenty of land in India for people to live on. It is so rich a country. Why are people worried?'

A child with a broom as minute as herself swept up dust in the courtyard, the bristles whispering in the dust. 'Children should be a joy and a pleasure,' Mother Teresa whispered,

'I am not trying to stop people from having children. I am only trying to ensure that they plan them, so that it is a joyful occasion when a child is born.' Her wrinkled face had the peace of certitude. She was very still as she talked, economic with her energy when it was not necessary to use it to any purpose. I did not agree with very much that she said, but I didn't say so. There seemed no point in arguing with a saint, even if one wished that saints were more of this world.

The Dalai Lama

It was raining again. In the gardens of Hyderabad House the lilac bushes dripped softly; water trickled through the channels of the rockeries and overflowed the normally arid bowls of the fountains. The great house which contained the Dalai Lama stood patiently in the middle distance, being rained on.

I saw all this from outside, through the great gates guarded by Sikh soldiers. Several tents had been pitched on the grass verge of the road to accommodate them and the security officers. A tangle of barbed wire lay, for no apparent purpose, in the grass: the Sikhs came carefully round it as the car drew up at the gate, and asked for my pass.

'I haven't got one.'

'Ha!' one of them said triumphantly. 'Then you cannot enter.'

'I have an appointment.'

'You must see the security officer,' the Sikh said.

So I climbed gingerly out into the rain and was led to a tent where a sad man sat with a telephone at his elbow. He picked this telephone up after I had put my case to him, and gloomily asked it for the private secretary. In a little while the telephone spoke volubly to him. At the end he nodded and put the receiver distastefully back on the hook.

'You are expected. The private secretary will meet you in the entrance. You may not take your car.'

I went back with the soldier who had brought me. He unlocked the gate and let me into the grounds. Then he trotted behind me, extending a small black umbrella that mushroomed from his fist over my head. A second soldier followed carrying the first one's rifle. In this manner, somewhat like a military funeral, we passed down the puddled driveway into the great porch.

A lama in brown robes stood in the porch. He was tall and elderly, and kept his hands in his sleeves. A rosary hung out of one sleeve. He said without pleasure, in English, 'I am the private secretary. Come inside.' We went into the entrance hall. Hyderabad House is now a state guest house, but it was formerly the Delhi palace of the Nizam, and the entrance hall is clearly the entrance hall of a palace: a huge domed roof, marble flooring, and grubby statues everywhere. Several groups of lamas, some in brown robes, some in black, stood talking softly under the dome that filtered a submarine light into the hall beneath. Their rosaries clicked softly. The private secretary deposited me on a sofa and went swimming away from me with prodigious strides, his robes floating about him. A young lama approached and sat, a little shyly, at my side.

He asked, in excellent English, if I had come to see His Holiness. Yes, I said. Was I a journalist? I denied this. He suddenly laughed and shook a finger at me: 'Ah, I see it, you are a poet. I see it by your hair.'

To change the subject I asked him where he had learnt his English. He had been to school in India, he said. 'Then this isn't your first visit?'

'No, indeed, but I hope it will be the last.'

'Why?'

He shrugged and wouldn't answer.

I asked him if he had come out with the Dalai Lama. He said yes. 'That was a terrible trip,' he said, 'a terrible trip. I do not like to remember.'

At this point the private secretary came hurrying back with a harassed-looking Indian official and a slender young Sikkimese in a bush-shirt. The lama beside me vanished, and the official sat down in his place and said emphatically: 'You understand that the condition on which this audience has been granted is that you should ask no political questions?' I nodded. 'Please keep to that condition. Now, there are certain other things. Do not touch His Holiness. That is sacrilege. When the audience is terminated, do not turn your back on His Holiness. Leave the room backwards. Also, kindly do not ask His Holiness rude questions.'

'How do you mean, rude questions?'

'Do not ask His Holiness if he believes that he is a god.'

'It had never occurred to me to do so,' I said truthfully.

'Very well.' He beckoned to the Sikkimese. 'This gentleman is your interpreter. Please remember that he will not translate political questions. His Holiness will now receive you.'

The interpreter led me out of the entrance hall through a carpeted corridor that emerged on a square courtyard. This courtyard had taken on the air of a lamasery already: groups of lamas stood about talking in the entrance hall, and two or three sat on rugs turning prayer-wheels. The drone of their prayers came to me through the rain-cooled air. The interpreter paused at a doorway on one side of the courtyard, whispering to me, 'Prepare yourself.' Then he turned into the room, and I followed.

It was a big drawing-room, full of sofas and occasional tables, and looking over the garden. In the middle of acres of carpet the Dalai Lama stood smiling. From his photographs I had always got the impression of somebody with an elongated body and enormous head: I was surprised to find him actually a sturdy, broad-shouldered, tall young man. He had clear skin and rosy cheeks, and wore black-rimmed pince-nez, slightly inappropriate-looking on the young face. His brown robe was open at the neck to reveal a tan shirt. He came forward and gave me an extremely firm handshake. The interpreter fluttered and kept trying to entice us to various sofas. Finally the Dalai Lama chose one by the window, pointed firmly to it, and turned to me, smiling. He gestured and said in English, 'Please sit.'

It was an enormous sofa. I sank into it with trepidation. The Dalai Lama sat beside me and the interpreter drew up a chair facing us. The Dalai Lama crossed his legs composedly, revealing under the robe brown brogues and a pair of red socks with yellow stripes. He spoke first. His voice was deep and clear, and he spoke rather fast, giving an impression of tremendous eagerness. He spoke in Tibetan, but looked at me all the while with brown intelligent eyes.

'His Holiness would much like to read some of your poetries,' said the interpreter. 'Is it possible for you to send him some poetries?'

'Yes, certainly. Has His Holiness read a great deal of literature then, apart from Tibetan literature?'

This was translated, and the Dalai Lama shook his head emphatically, the corners of his mouth turned down in a charming and rueful smile. I felt this was an answer, and was surprised when the interpreter began, rather hurriedly, to translate: 'His Holiness is familiar with all the literatures of the world.'

I asked, ignoring this fatuity, 'Is there any secular literature in Tibet? The recent revolt, for instance, did that produce any literature?'

The interpreter translated this. He addressed the Dalai Lama as 'Kundun,' his usual Tibetan title, which means 'Presence'. As he ended each sentence he sketched a little obeisance with hand and head. Kundun thought carefully, and then answered.

'His Holiness says that he does not know of any literature, but there may be some. The difficulty about finding out would be that such literature manuscripts will be in Tibet and not India.'

'If they could be found I would like to try and translate them, if His Holiness feels that their publication in the West would help the Tibetan cause.'

The Dalai Lama nodded when this was translated, and smiled with his vivid smile. He leant forward, tapped me on the knee, and said something. 'His Holiness thanks you for your interest in the Tibetan people. He hopes to be able to send some of the young men of his people to your university, to Oxford, and to other Western universities. He will see if he is able to afford, and if possible he will send.'

'Does His Holiness not feel that young men brought up in an exclusively Eastern society in Tibet may have difficulty in the West?'

The Dalai Lama surprisingly began to answer this before it was translated. He shook his head emphatically at the start, then went on, talking quickly with many gestures of one long, capable hand, and occasionally reaching over to tap me on the knee. He smiled all the while, but usually a little wryly, the corners of his mouth turned down; it was only when he was genuinely amused or interested that the corners of the mouth lifted, the cheeks got pinker, and the eyes gleamed. Now he was explaining something unpleasant, and the smile was downturned.

'His Holiness says that the Chinese have already altered the structure of Tibetan society and introduced Western things. They have done this by force and brutality but they have altered Tibet in a way that has made it impossible for Tibetans to return entirely to their old system. Tibet will have to turn more and more to the West.'

I recalled the Dalai Lama's flight from Lhasa. 'When His Holiness left the Potala, we were told there was a great dust storm that prevented the Chinese from seeing him. Some people have suggested that this dust storm was sent by Providence. Does His Holiness agree?'

His Holiness shrugged his shoulders, and said something.

'Kundun says that there are many dust storms in Tibet at that season.'

I laughed at this. The Dalai Lama laughed too and again tapped me gently on the knee. 'How did His Holiness feel during the flight?'

This was answered briefly: 'Nervous.'

'Can His Holiness remember his childhood before he was chosen as Lama?'

The Dalai Lama nodded.

'Does he have any clear memories of it? Did he feel any different to other children?'

The Dalai Lama looked thoughtful at this. The long hands moved as though sketching a childhood in the air. But he shook his head.

'His Holiness has no particular memory of that part of his life. He cannot tell if he felt any different from other children, because he had no standards of comparison. But his mother always said that he was the noisiest child she had ever seen.'

The Dalai Lama watched me closely throughout the translation. When the interpreter reached the last sentence, an expectant gleam came into his eyes, and when I laughed he joined delightedly in the laughter. He leant forward and said something to the interpreter.

'Kundun asks if you have any more questions.'

'Not if he doesn't want any more.'

The Dalai Lama looked pleased when this was translated. He smiled, rubbed his hands together boyishly, and spoke again to the translator.

'His Holiness says it is good that you have no more questions because now you can both talk properly. He says he is sorry he does not speak English, he is learning, but as yet he cannot speak it well. He asks you what you studied at Oxford.'

I said literature. The Dalai Lama nodded. The next question was about the methods of instruction. I explained the tutorial system. Again he nodded.

'Kundun thinks this is a good method. He asks you to describe the life in Oxford.'

So I found myself explaining scouts, landladies, the importance of the pub, the bicycle, and the river. The Dalai Lama listened to all this closely, occasionally stopping me to put in various questions. What was a punt? What academic dress did people wear? Why were colleges locked at midnight? Finally he made a quick switch of topic.

'Kundun wishes to know to how many countries you have been?'

And, after I had given him a list, 'How many languages can you speak?' As this was translated the Dalai Lama leant across to me and interjected inquiringly: 'Spanish?'

I shook my head. 'French, Italian, a little German, a little Greek.'

The Dalai Lama, seeming disappointed, asked again, 'Spanish no?'

'Tell His Holiness I can't speak Spanish. Why is he so interested in Spanish?'

'He has seen a book of pictures about Spain. It seems to him a very beautiful country. He wishes that he could visit Oxford and travel to European countries, especially to Spain.'

'Does he plan to travel a lot?'

The Dalai Lama for the first time looked sad. His hands lay inert in his lap as he spoke. 'Kundun says that he cannot be interested in travel except in so far as it will help his country. He may visit some of the Buddhist countries, and if the Tibetan case is brought before the United Nations he may go to America, but he will always make India his base, and always return to it, because it is near his country.'

The Dalai Lama now spoke again, slowly and sadly. His face was grim, shadowed, quiet. He spoke for a long time. When he had finished the interpreter looked nervous.

'I cannot translate that.'

The Dalai Lama leant across again, putting his hand on my knee, and spoke urgently and even a little imperiously to the interpreter, who shook his head respectfully. He was sorry, he could not translate. I was divided between irritation and nervousness: nervousness because I was sure that in allowing the Dalai Lama to tap me on the knee, I was committing some awful unconscious sacrilege. I kept edging unobtrusively away, but he had obligingly humped himself along in my wake, so that by now we had traversed the entire length of the sofa and I was more or less pinioned against the farther arm. I hoped no lamas would look in. There was not much of my thought left free for me to feel irritated with, but I managed.

'Can't you just give me the gist of what His Holiness is saying?'

And then suddenly, coldly, precisely, the Dalai Lama lifted his voice. He spoke only a few words, but the interpreter looked up into his face and hurriedly began to translate.

'Kundun says that there are many people not far from here who speak of peace, truth, and goodwill. They are constantly lecturing others about this. They make promises in the name of peace and goodwill, yet when the time comes to keep those promises, they are always broken. This is as great a danger as aggressive militarism, in a different way.'

He hesitated.

'Kundun says there are two great forces in the world today. One is the force of the people with power, with armies to enforce their power, and with a land to recruit their armies from. The other is the force of the poor and dispossessed. The two are in perpetual conflict, and it is certain who will lose.'

The Dalai Lama added something to this. The interpreter again hesitated, but catching the Dalai Lama's eye stumbled on into a very curious remark.

'His Holiness says that this is the reason why there are so many suicides in the world today.'

There was a silence. The Dalai Lama's grave, stooped face did not change. I said rather lamely, 'That is quite true.'

The Dalai Lama spoke again. The interpreter said, 'Unless this is changed, the world will perish, Kundun says. Therefore every poet, every religious man, every political leader, should fight against this division till he dies. The teachings of the Lord Buddha also tell us this.'

'How does he think poets should do this?'

The Dalai Lama launched into a long, obviously detailed answer. He emphasized each point with a tap on my knee. His forehead wrinkled a little with concentration, when he had finished, I asked, 'What did Kundun say?'

The interpreter, looking baffled, replied, 'He says poets must insert references to Tibet in their poems.'

The Dalai Lama shook his head helplessly at me, and suddenly laughed. We both laughed together once more, which was nice. I realized that I had been there for more than an hour, and that I should go. We all stood up and the Dalai Lama dropped his arm round my shoulders in a friendly gesture. He came quite close. I saw that the Dalai Lama had freckles on his nose.

He shook my hand with the same firm clasp as before, and stepped aside. I remembered what I had been told about not turning my back. I accordingly began to sidle out backward, crab-fashion. The Dalai Lama watched me for a moment. Then he suddenly took a few steps forward, dropped his hands to my shoulders, and turned me round so that I faced the door. He gave me a friendly push to speed me on my way. I heard his laugh behind me, for the last time.

Outside the door the grim black-robed elder lamas were standing, rosaries in their gnarled fingers. I looked back. Kundun was standing alone in the middle of the room as he had done when I came in. I waved at him across all those acres of carpet. He waved back, and briefly the beautiful smile came again to his face. Then I went away.